Advance Praise for *Dementia Sucks*

"When I face the challenges in my life, I use journaling as an outlet for my thoughts and emotions. Never before have I read someone else's, until now. *Dementia Sucks* is a revealing journal-based story exploring the rapid decline Alzheimer's brings about. For all the horror of this disease, the journey of this book reveals something beautiful. You will discover the humanity, the joy, and the hope that is ever present, even in the darkest hour with tears streaming down your face."

—Mike Michalowicz,
author of *Profit First*

"*Dementia Sucks* says it all in two words. But if you are looking for answers to what is happening with someone you know who seems to be in slow mental descent, or has been diagnosed with dementia, Tracey S. Lawrence has left a brave, revealing and valuable diary in your path. Pick it up and read it. You will find humor, pain, honesty, answers, and proof you are not alone. It is on one hand a manual for the multitudes coming to grips with this broad category of brain disease, on the other a love story. Thank you Tracey for sharing your courageous tale."

—Gary Donatelli, producer of
23 Blast and director of *One Life to Live*

D_EMEN_TIA SU_CKS

A CAREGIVER'S JOURNEY · WITH LESSONS LEARNED

TRACEY S. LAWRENCE

Post Hill
PRESS

A POST HILL PRESS BOOK

ISBN: 978-1-68261-671-0
ISBN (eBook): 978-1-68261-672-7

Dementia Sucks
A Caregiver's Journey—With Lessons Learned
© 2018 by Tracey S. Lawrence
All Rights Reserved

Cover art by Cody Corcoran

Post Hill Press
New York • Nashville
posthillpress.com

Published in the United States of America

For Roz and Herb

CONTENTS

INTRODUCTION:
SPRING 2017

Upon hearing my story, many people I meet have suggested I write a book. My usual response to that idea has been, "Sure. When I have time. Ha ha ha." And being the ever-busy, multiple-hat-wearing person I am, the time didn't seem right. Until now.

I've always been a writer. Any time I've been in emotional distress and needed an outlet, writing has been my refuge. I have kept numerous journals throughout my life. They have always been private and I have never shared them with anyone. They are my personal ravings. No one else needs to read them.

Caregiving my mother changed that.

I had taken my mother into my home in northern New Jersey to live with my husband and me when it became clear she could no longer live independently, in April 2010. When I brought my mother back to her apartment in Florida in October of that year, I knew it was the beginning of the end for her. And being alone with her for so many hours in that depressing apartment she and my father had once shared, I felt the acute need to write. And I thought, maybe what I'm learning here could have value for others. What the hell? I'll create a blog.

I kept it going from October 2010 until my mother's passing in April 2015. I didn't realize quite how much I had recorded.

Upon review, it dawned on me that the book I needed to write was pretty much written. It just needed some polish.

Looking back, it's interesting to observe how much I'd forgotten. I'm glad I documented what happened. It's good to be able to appreciate all we were able to overcome.

I think it's also important for readers to understand why this is written in the "present tense" when it's so clearly my history. While I felt compelled to clean up the original material, I didn't think it necessary to disguise that it was derived from journal entries. It's more real, honest, and immediate in its original form.

During the course of this journey, I was compelled to start a business applying what I learned in the service of others. I'm not here to sell you anything. But if you come away with anything from reading this, I hope it will be, at bare minimum, that illness is a family affair, and being proactive can save your life.

Denial is human. Procrastination is too. But so is dementia. And long-lasting illness. And death. You can prepare for it, or take it as it comes. Believe me when I tell you that dementia really does suck. But it sucks a lot less when you've planned for it.

Read my story. Understand that this doesn't just happen to other people. It happens to most of us in some form.

And if you're one of the lucky ones to whom it does not happen, please let me know how you did it so I can share your secret with others.

—Tracey

CHAPTER 1:
DROWNING IN STUFF

October 10, 2010

Bob, Mom and Me, Easter 2009

As my mother's mental state continues to deteriorate, I cling to my own sanity, trying to make some sense of what's happening to her. She is eighty-one years old.

Having lived on her own in southeastern Florida following the death of my father in July 2004, in time it became clear that she was not functioning well. Money she withdrew from the bank kept disappearing and turning up in places like her clothes hamper. She claimed there was no heat in her apartment when it got cold, but I now suspect that she simply didn't know how to turn it on.

In February 2010, I brought Mom north to try living in a senior apartment twenty minutes from my home in Ringwood, New Jersey. (A small jewel of a town at the northeastern border of the state, Ringwood is about 40 miles from midtown Manhattan. It gives me access to the city I love as needed, while affording me the joy of spending my days surrounded by trees, mountains, lakes, critters, and fresh air.) She tried it out for a few months. I took her furniture shopping to make the place more comfortable and homey. She still hated it and complained that it was too expensive. I took her to look at other places, and she finally admitted that she would prefer to live with my husband, Bob, and me.

Living with us had been the first option I had offered her, and we had tried it in 2009 for four months as she recuperated from the removal of her gallbladder. She didn't want to "intrude" on us, so once she felt well enough, she returned to Florida. Defusing her initial resistance, I hired an aide to help her four hours a day, five days a week. Mom actually enjoyed the freedom of having a "personal assistant," but the caregiver soon found a full-time job elsewhere and Mom didn't want to try another one. Her attempt at resuming unaided independent living wasn't working.

As I had told her the first time around, of all the lousy options available, living with us was the option that sucked the least. In April 2010, Mom moved into our guest bedroom, and we've been acclimating, making changes to the house, seeking legal estate advice, providing her with a space heater to keep her room a balmy 90 degrees, and getting her medical needs met.

We still have to deal with her apartment. Fortunately, Dad left her in good shape financially, and we aren't pressured to sell her place immediately. It's a co-op with a great view and fairly low maintenance costs. It is filled with artwork, bric-a-brac, clothes, and remnants of the once-happy consumer frenzy my parents enjoyed together. I've brought Mom down to deal with some of it. Sort, identify what might have value up north, throw out what's expired, useless, or shot, give away what might have value for others, and leave what makes the apartment functional when we need to be there.

My folks bought this two-bedroom, two-bath split on the fourteenth floor overlooking the Intracoastal and Atlantic Ocean beyond in 1987 for eighty-five thousand dollars. At the height of the market ten years ago, similar apartments sold for 350 thousand dollars. Then the crash of 2008 sent the values into the toilet. Comparable apartments now go for about 150 thousand dollars. I think we'll sit for a while, but we still have to start dealing with all this *stuff.*

Mom did give away most of Dad's clothes and personal effects within the first year after his passing. But there is still so much accumulated junk in the five walk-in closets, it's overwhelming. And Mom needs to go through her clothes. She needs warmer items to wear up north as winter approaches. She's lost considerable weight over the last year or so. The gallbladder surgery forced her to curtail the amount of food she ate, and later, she experienced toxicity from all her medications. I got her prescriptions adjusted, and she's on less than half the pills she was before. Losing weight addressed many of the conditions from which she had been suffering, so she needs a lot less medication. But now we need to figure out what fits her and what doesn't.

The big problem is that she constantly misplaces things. I have managed to narrow down this problem to four reasons: 1) her eyesight is questionable, 2) she spaces out and compulsively puts things together that don't really belong together, 3) she doesn't like to throw things away, 4) she has *way* too much *stuff*.

Having dealt with my father's dementia seven years ago, I've educated myself about the disease, and I'm confident Mom doesn't have Alzheimer's.[1] Day to day, she knows what's going on and remembers important events. She forgets names. She misplaces important items and gets agitated when she can't find things. She's easily distracted. However, she's not paranoid; she knows it's her and she does trust me. So it could be worse.

Meanwhile, I'm trying to keep her on track, focused on the tasks at hand. She avoids my repeated requests that she try on clothes so we can figure out what items should go north, and what should get donated or chucked. It isn't easy, but as my dear father once opined, no one said it was going to be.

---

[1]   I was wrong. Mom did, in fact, have Alzheimer's disease.

CHAPTER 2:
OH, CRAP

October 11, 2010

One of the few pleasures I have when I'm down here in Florida is swimming in the pool. It's not exactly Olympic-sized, but it's convenient, refreshing, and situated right on the Intracoastal Waterway. And as any caregiver worth her salt can tell you, finding the time for regular exercise is especially important.

Today, after I finished up with Mom for the morning, she was settling in for an afternoon nap, and I went down to the pool. A fellow in a maintenance uniform was opening an industrial-sized barrel of chemicals. I figured he was doing regular pool upkeep. As I walked toward an umbrella table to put down my things, the pool guy looks up at me and tells me I can't swim. "Somebody pooped." He went on to inform me that he was going to put an extra-heavy dose of chemicals in the pool and that there would be no swimming for another two to three days. Just in time for our departure.

Huh boy.

Not wishing to have my fitness thwarted by such a disgusting impediment, I went back upstairs, changed my clothes, and went to walk along the Hollywood Beach Boardwalk. I saw sailboats on the Atlantic. I observed the changes to the local bistros, parks, and hotels.

Tomorrow, I think I'll rent a bike (weather permitting).

When I got back, Mom had actually gone through her clothes; she's pared down the cache of winter clothes she wants to bring back north. Progress has been made.

In spite of the challenges presented earlier in the day, I suppose we could mark this day as being flushed with success.

CHAPTER 3:
FALSE ALARM

October 12, 2010

Mom likes to hold on to old drugs. She has bottles of my father's prescription painkillers that expired before he did. She keeps them "just in case." I sneak these into the trash whenever I can without her noticing.

The other day, I had been sitting out on the terrace, reading. I walked into the kitchen and spotted a scrap of paper on the kitchen table. On it was inscribed a very sad poem in my mother's handwriting. The words were of love and loss. The last line was "Goodbye." On the table, next to the note, were some empty pill bottles which had once contained Valium and oxycodone.

Now, Mom has been depressed since Dad died six years ago. She has expressed the wish that her life would end. Her morbid attitude was one of the driving reasons for bringing her to live with us in the first place. I know in my heart she doesn't have it in her to end her life by her own hand. However, doing the math (note + empty pill bottles + closed bedroom door), I got a little nervous and walked into Mom's bedroom.

I observed Mom sleeping on the bed. She was breathing normally. I went in and touched her arm. She opened her eyes.

"Everything okay, Mom?"

She responded in the affirmative. I went back to the kitchen to retrieve the note and I showed it to her. She put on her glasses, looked at it, and explained that she had been trying to recall the lyrics of an old favorite torch song from the days of the Dorsey Brothers. Then she sang the song. Mom still has a pretty voice.

CHAPTER 4:
SUPERNATURAL

October 13, 2010

The preponderance of horror/fantasy entertainment in our culture at the moment is striking. Consider how many vampire vehicles there are (I'm a "Truebie"[2] myself). This genre also tends to include werewolves and other exotic creatures of the night.

Then there's the zombie genre. Beginning with *Night of the Living Dead*, there've been many variations on this theme, including a Cartoon Central comedy series and a feature starring Jesse Eisenberg and Woody Harrelson called *Zombieland*.

When you consider how many people in this country are my age (born in the late '50s) and how many of us are caring for our aging parents, it's no surprise that escapist entertainments are providing us distraction and comic relief.

It occurred to me this morning that aging parents are kind of like zombies. (Note to the PC police: don't harangue me about pejoratively classifying old people as "zombies." Read on before you decide). They start out human, but later morph into something else that can be truly frightening. Because they *look* like our parents, we tend treat them as we always have. However, much as we may love these creatures,

---

2   *True Blood* was an HBO series I had enjoyed for its first several seasons. The last few, not so much.

their quality of life depends on our ability to discern what they're becoming, and that we modify our attitudes and reactions in appropriate ways.

And I find that, like Jesse Eisenberg's character in *Zombieland*, if you intend to survive, you need to establish some rules to live by:

- **Get organized.** If you know where important items are, you are more likely to be able to save the day by locating what he or she is looking for before he or she totally freaks out.
- **Write stuff down.** You're remembering for two (or more) now. I find my iPod Touch[3] to be invaluable. You can store everything in one place and there are no scraps of paper to lose. (Just don't lose the device, and back it up regularly in case you do.)
- **Pay attention to new behaviors.** If something weird happens once, it might just be an aberration. Twice begins a pattern that may reveal a new issue.
- **Get support.** When you care for someone on your own, you will eventually need to talk to other rational people. You will need perspective. Depending on the relationship you have with your parent, you may need help changing the dynamic. It's natural for families to resume the traditional roles they've played with one another when they reunite after a long period of independent life. We outgrow these old roles and must grow into new

---

[3]   This was before I had an iPhone. My electronic note-taking continues.

ones that work for the phase to come. And they will keep evolving.

- **Get your parent a good geriatric physician who will partner with you.**
- **Unplug.** Take breaks whenever you can. You need to remember who you are and what you need.
- **Find humor in your situation.**
- **Find healthy ways of dealing with your stress and maintaining your own health.**
- **Adapt.** Keep adding to your list of rules.

This is a process that many people are going through. If we find each other, stick together, and share our experiences, we can stem the tide of despair and find our way to the next phase, until we begin our own inevitable transformations. I don't intend to become a zombie. But who ever did?

CHAPTER 5:
HAPPY HOLIDAYS

December 1, 2010

Happy Hanukkah. It's been a while since my last install-ment. On the heels of Thanksgiving, I know we have much for which to be thankful. Some days, it's so hard to genuinely *feel* that.

Since our return from Florida, the renovations to our home are just about complete. We now have a hot tub right behind our bedroom. This was high on my husband's wish list, and I found the resources to make it happen. It is a very relaxing, therapeutic device. And our nieces really enjoyed it when they came for Thanksgiving. I personally couldn't see the value of getting into a vat of 104-degree water and then emerging into 30-degree air, but it's actually nice. And the massage is awesome, particularly for my feet and shoulders.

When we first got home, my brother called and told me he'd read my blog (that was surprising) and he felt bad. He offered to take Mom to his house for the weekend to give us a break. We took him up on it. It was nice to have some time to ourselves. It wasn't nearly enough, but you take what you can get.

Clearly, he didn't exactly enjoy her visit, and my brother's comment upon their return was typical: "No one held a gun to your head." Don't blame me. I never asked you to do this.

Well, quite true, no one did. And truth be told, this is, on many levels, a nightmare come to life. But what options are there? Having explored so many, this was what we'd come up with. Should we have left her in Florida to fend for herself? Left her in the senior apartment where her needs were not being met and I was *still* left holding the bag for her doctor appointments and administrative stuff? Painful as this is, it's still the most workable situation.

I did decide to approach her doctor with the possibility that my mother is depressed and suffering from pseudo-dementia rather than the real thing.[4] After examining her, he agreed and put her on an antidepressant. It's too soon to tell if it's working (it can take as long as twelve weeks), but she's only been on the drug for four weeks and it doesn't seem to be doing any harm.

Meanwhile, Bob and I try to keep talking to each other. We snap at each other more than we used to, but we know each other well enough to understand why we're doing it. Talking calmly, taking timeouts for ourselves, and soaking in the tub help a lot.

I've also just joined an online support group for caregivers. It's nice to read what others are going through. One woman's post made me tear up in recognition. Others make

---

4   I knew about pseudo-dementia because of my father. His dementia was never accurately diagnosed by a medical professional, but "pseudo-dementia due to depression" was one of the many diagnoses proffered by a neurologist who examined him. My observations, knowledge of his medical history, and research led me to conclude that he suffered from vascular dementia, related to his coronary artery disease. The constant changes in his symptoms corresponded to likely TIAs or "mini-strokes" affecting different areas of his brain.

me feel like I don't have it so bad. It just underscores the importance of community. This is clearly why religions developed. This is the new religion for our time: Welcome to The Church of Online Support.

And now, having put the finishing touches on my post, I'm going to go work out and prepare to televise my town's council meetings.

Happy Holidays, folks. May you get what you need and enjoy what you get.

CHAPTER 6:
WELCOME TO STAGE VI

December 5, 2010

Up until now, Mom's been mostly "forgetful," but functional. She knew where she was and what she was doing with me in my house. In the last couple of days, she's clearly crossed over to the next level.

The other day, she was struggling to remember how to make ice water. She couldn't figure out how to tie her shoelaces. She put on two different shoes or left one off altogether. She sleeps in her clothes.

And she's hallucinating. She's waiting to see her long-dead father. She's been searching for Grady, our beloved cat who died more than a year ago.

Saturday evening, when Bob and I reluctantly left Mom alone to go to a concert in Manhattan with friends, I called from a restaurant to check on her. She answered the phone on the first ring and was freaking out. She reported that there were people all over the house playing loud music and having parties. She described seeing overpasses and trestles. She was afraid to leave her "apartment" because she might trip the alarm and upset "Dan" downstairs. (We live in a one-family home.) I calmly asked if she could find her way to the bedroom. She said she thought she could. I encouraged her to find the bed and lay down until we could get home to her.

We cut our evening short and I drove home like a maniac. Upon our return, I found Mom flopped on her bed, in her clothes, kind of half on, half hanging off. She opened her eyes when I rubbed her arm and she asked if I'd seen her husband (Dad died in 2004, and when reminded, she usually knows it). She also asked me if I had joined a cult.

I knew she wasn't going to get better, but it's still kind of a shock to witness such a sudden decline.

Thank goodness Mom has long-term care insurance. She's going to need it.

CHAPTER 7:
NEW MEDICATION, POSSIBLE REVELATION

December 7, 2010

I took Mom to her doctor today and had her relate the story of her adventures in "the wrong apartment." I cited some of her other peculiar new behaviors, and she seemed puzzled. She thought I might be "embellishing." The doctor suggested returning to Aricept, but that medication had given her pretty intense gastric symptoms, so we'd stopped it.

He offered a product called Exelon patch, which is similar to Aricept, but it's absorbed through the skin, so it's less likely to cause stomach problems. Tomorrow, we start slapping those puppies on her. He plans to add Namenda to the mix once we see how she does on these.

When we got home, Mom went into the kitchen and looked at pictures she had attached to the refrigerator. These prints I had made for her were scanned from images taken of her and my father when they were middle-aged and having a nice time at a nightclub. She looked at them and chastised Herby for not living longer.

Then something occurred to me. Lately, she has begun to use symbolic language to express things for which she can't find more appropriate words. She also appears to be acting out in ways that she can't control. She keeps separating her shoes and socks, putting one shoe of a pair in the closet and the other in a drawer. Perhaps this is her way of communicating that feeling of loss. She's the unmatched shoe of a fifty-three-year-old pair.

CHAPTER 8:
IT'S NOT A
LINEAR PATH

December 9, 2010

Mom's first hired caregiver started yesterday. I got the two of them situated, giving Mom a bunch of photo albums so she could acquaint her new "friend" with her family. I took the opportunity to work in my office with one ear pointed toward the living room. It went fine.

The bizarre behaviors (mismatched shoes) and hallucinations have abated, but the confusion and forgetfulness are ever-present. She attempted to repair an open seam on the comforter on her bed yesterday, but she kept forgetting what she was doing and gave up.

Mom retains the vivid memory of her adventures in "the apartment" from Saturday, but last night after dinner she told me that she realized how ridiculous the story sounded in retrospect. She also remembers that she's on a new medication and wants to ensure she takes it properly. I helped her find her shower cap and she's taking a shower without assistance as I write. Her caregiver just arrived, and I have to go see one of my clients. It will be interesting to see how she does while I'm out of the house.

My dad's dementia fluctuated; having vascular dementia, his symptoms were constantly changing as mini-strokes went off in his brain. Sometimes, he'd be completely lucid. I referred to these episodes as his "visits." Other times, he'd be interacting with phantoms only he could see. The consistent thing was his obvious misery.

Chances are Mom's dementia is something else, but it sure isn't linear. Symptoms come and go. The severity of her confusion varies. She can even make jokes about her forgetfulness. It's a meandering journey. It's life.

CHAPTER 9:
DEMENTIA IS CONTAGIOUS

December 14, 2010

One of the most frustrating things about caring for someone with dementia is that they're completely inconsistent. Sometimes, they actually do know what they're talking about. Occasionally, you'll be the one who inadvertently misplaces some sought-after object. You're so busy trying to remember everything you need, everything *they* need, and trying to keep yourself from punching anyone, it's easy to become overwhelmed.

Over the weekend, Mom was commenting on our neighbor's holiday display across the street. She remarked about how it kept changing. I assumed it was just the difference between the way the house looked by day and by night. Mom is blind in one eye from macular degeneration, and I assumed it was her bad eyesight combined with failing cognition.

Then Bob went to the local liquor store and spoke to our neighbor, John, from across the street, who works there. John asked Bob how Mom was doing. The topic of Mom's perception of their holiday display came up. John then told Bob that his sister did indeed change the display each day! Mom has time to stare out the window and observe little details. I don't. She was absolutely correct!

We were sitting on the sofa and admiring our tree the first night it was up. As the lights flashed, I mentioned that we will probably be replacing our artificial tree with a new one next season. It still looks nice, but it drops a lot of flotsam (like a real tree). Mom asked if there were any restrictions on the type of tree we could have in "the apartment." I reminded her that we owned our home and could do as we pleased in that regard. She remarked that the bank owned our home and I readily agreed with that assessment.

I found her glasses in the shower. Her missing plastic cup turned up under her bed. The bright pink shower cap I bought her was under a pile of other junk in one of her storage towers.

Then the supermarket calls to confirm my order and asks if there's anything I'd like to add. Uhhhhhhh...

My head hurts, I'm tired, and I have menstrual cramps. Can I *please* have a day off and get my brain back for my own personal use and amusement?

CHAPTER 10:
HAPPY NEW YEAR

January 4, 2011

Mom and Max recover from the holiday hub-bub

We had a wonderful, if hectic, Christmas. My three nieces (identical twins and their younger, college-student sister) and two of their boyfriends came in waves, starting Friday, Christmas Eve. The plan was for the girls and their guys to stay two nights, and then head down to south Jersey on Sunday for a party with the other side of their family. Two nieces and one boyfriend would be returning on Monday as the youngest had an interview at Columbia University on Tuesday for a summer job as a resident assistant. I offered to take her to the appointment.

A major blizzard extended their stay through Tuesday. It was great having five twenty-somethings around to help shovel us out from more than two feet of snow. We also had a swell time playing games and soaking in the hot tub. It was a particular blast being in the tub during the height of the storm!

The girls are very sweet with Mom. The youngest engages her in conversation easily. They brought her a gift basket full of goodies too. Mom enjoyed herself to the extent that she could, but the noise and tumult were confusing. And her ability to eat unassisted is evaporating.

We had planned on meeting my brother and his family for brunch on that Sunday, but the storm started around 11 a.m., so they didn't make it. But we got Mom up and out and we all went out to a local tavern for brunch ahead of the blizzard. I ordered Mom a dish she could eat mostly with her hands, and that worked out pretty well.

On Tuesday, one of the twins and her boyfriend left, our hired caregiver arrived to stay with Mom, and the rest of us struck out for Columbia University. I got to spend time with the remaining twin while the youngest had her interview (and was hired on the spot!). Once we got back to Ringwood, the girls and the remaining boyfriend took off for Maryland. The house returned to "normal." I got to work doing lots of laundry and vacuuming.

Meanwhile, the nurse who was charged with evaluating Mom's condition for her long-term care claim thought it best to delay her Tuesday appointment until Thursday because of the snow. As the days passed, my concern that Mom's symptoms would abate upon the nurse's arrival evolved to worry that keeping her here with us might not be practical for the long term.

On Thursday, the nurse arrived a little late (GPS issues), but she was kind and clearly knew her business. Mom knew the year, but not the month or date. She didn't know what street she lived on or the name of the town. She couldn't copy a line drawing of two intersecting pentagons. When asked to write down a sentence, after an agonizing interval, she copied a sentence that appeared higher up on the page. I reported some of Mom's issues for the record and we discussed items that might facilitate Mom's care. As she was leaving, I asked the nurse if there was any doubt about the legitimacy of Mom's claim. She said "not at all" and recommended some resources for me.

For New Year's Eve, I prepared the prime rib roast I'd bought on sale. I cooked it nice and rare the way Bob and Mom like. I cut up Mom's rib into bite-sized chunks, but left all the pieces assembled around the bone so it looked whole.

Mom had been dressed all day as the caregiver had been with her. When I announced it was dinner time, Mom went into her room and decided to remove her top and bra and partially put on a flannel nightgown. She had one arm through, backwards, and the rest of her was hanging out as she approached the dining room. I guided her into the bathroom, got her fully into the gown, and helped her back to the table.

She didn't touch her salad and didn't seem to know how to approach the meat. She'd pick up pieces with her fingers, chew them, drop them on the floor. I went over and helped cut the meat into smaller pieces. She remarked that she would soon need a high chair.

Eventually, she gave up and went to bed.

Bob tried to comfort me as I cleaned up.

We watched some TV.

As midnight approached, Bob prepared the champagne and glasses. He opened the hot tub. We got in and listened for the countdown on TV. Bob popped open the bottle and poured. We drank, kissed, and watched the fireworks deployed by our reveling neighbors.

Bob asked what I wanted for the New Year. I said, "The strength to deal with what's coming."

Happy New Year, indeed.

CHAPTER 11:
MOM'S "VISIT"

January 8, 2011

Late Thursday afternoon, Mom's new Exelon patches arrived and I applied one right away. She'd apparently been having a pretty good day, taking better care of her appearance than she had been. She ate well at dinner. She stayed up and watched *Gorillas in the Mist* with me until 10. (Lately, she'd been going to bed right after dinner.)

This morning, we woke to significant snowfall. I wasn't feeling well (my periods always arrive with debilitating cramps and I have a mild sinus infection) and stayed in bed a little later than usual. When I rose, Mom was awake, dressed, and clear-eyed.

Mom's hired caregiver called. She was having problems getting out of her street (she lives on the other side of our mountainous town). I had already postponed my appointments for the day and told her to stay safe at home.

All day today, Mom's been a lot more like her old self. She put on makeup and styled her hair. She went down the stairs to answer the door and to search for cat treats for her furry "grandson." She even offered to bring me beverages as I rested.

So here's my question: what the hell is going on? Is this just the nature of the dementia beast? Could it be the medication? The vitamins and supplements I've been giving her? Better diet? Or maybe seeing me feeling poorly made her motherly impulses re-emerge?

When my dad was in the throes of his dementia, he had brief periods of remarkable lucidity. I'd call these his "visits." So today appears to be a "visit" from Mom. It would be nice if she could stick around for a while. It will be really interesting to see who shows up here tomorrow.

CHAPTER 12:
HELD OVER BY POPULAR DEMAND

January 17, 2011

It had been a week and Mom continued to be a lot more "Mom-like." Friday night, my brother, sister-in-law, and youngest nephew came up to meet us for dinner at a local restaurant. I told my brother Mom had been doing better, but seeing is believing.

I helped her with her clothing selections because some of her sweaters had little stains she couldn't see. (I put them in the wash.) She did her makeup and hair herself (I helped with the back). She even put her boots on unassisted.

My brother called to say he was on the way. We decided to meet at the restaurant so we could request a table for six and be seated shortly after their arrival. That strategy worked out well.

We sat down and looked over our menus. For the first time in many years, Mom ordered a cocktail. There had been times when she'd be up for a glass of white wine, but generally, she would go for water or tea. Last night, she asked for what my sister-in-law ordered (double vodka with cranberry) and we all looked at each other in shock. Then, without agonizing, she ordered chicken parmigiana with a lobster tail! Again, there was an exchange of surprised looks around the table.

Everyone (except my nine-year-old nephew, who is obsessed with video games and mostly attended to his iPad as the grown-ups conversed) ate and drank with gusto. Mom even laughed out loud a few times.

When we got home, Mom stayed up and watched TV with me. I passed out in my chair; she came over to kiss me good night and she went to bed.

In the morning, Mom got up a little later than usual (9:15 or so) and I asked her if she was hung over. She smiled and said she felt pretty good. I said it seemed like she had a really good time last night. She said she felt "human."

My brother called around 10 to say what a good time they had with us. He said Mom had told him she felt that she had been depressed and it was finally lifting. (When I spoke to her about it later, she had no recollection of that exchange.) I mentioned some of the changes I've been making to her regimen, including some supplements and better diet. The Exelon patches don't appear to be doing anything negative, and they may be helping to arrest the progress of her cognitive issues. And social interaction with caregivers has some obvious value as well.

As Sunday progressed, Mom's confusion became more profound again. When I told her that her usual caregiver would be back on Monday, she couldn't remember who that was, claiming to have only met her once (she had been coming here for more than two weeks). Mom's weekend caregiver tried to engage her in simple word games and puzzles. No interest there. No connection to the day of the week, even as she glanced at the Sunday paper.

As someone who has no innate sense of direction, I have learned to achieve a comfort level with being lost. It's been years since I've panicked over not knowing where I am; it's just part of the way I live my life. (I always carry maps in the car and my recent acquisition of a GPS device has been a boon in this regard.) But the point is, I'm glad to have a nature that allows me to stay calm despite seismic shifts. Another one is coming.

My birthday is on a Saturday this year and I hired coverage for that evening so I can go out with my husband without concern, my own birthday present to myself. Whether she needs it or not, it's good to know someone will be here.

One of my favorite expressions comes from Yiddish: "Man makes plans and God laughs." All I can do is prepare, and hope He'll let me in on the joke every now and then.

CHAPTER 13:
ON LYING

February 5, 2011

Lying is a practice I have always avoided. Aside from the fact that I lack a "poker face" (I flush, twitch, or exhibit a number of "tells" that inform anyone who's the tiniest bit observant of my discomfort), lying complicates life to a large extent.

My close friends can tell you I've always had a better-than-average memory. One of the reasons I've been able to keep my thoughts organized is *consistency*. Lying disrupts consistency. Having to remember what I said to whom would only further complicate my ability to manage the information in my head. When a lie is repeated often enough, the mind begins to accept it as "reality." I try to retain as much factual information (as I know it) as I can without muddying the waters any worse than they have been by the ravages of my own advancing age.

The exception to the lying rule, though, is Mom. The one person I have always felt compelled to lie to is my mother, because there are things a parent (mine in particular) does not want to know about their child (and vice versa). But this was a protective posture; she simply couldn't handle the truth (specifically about certain aspects of my life, like the fact that I am a sexually healthy person).

Now that Mom is advancing through dementia, there are times when my husband suggests I just humor her. Lie to her.

"Yes" her to death. But there's a problem with that. As I've mentioned previously, dementia does not progress in a linear fashion. There are things she does retain, particularly emotionally-charged ideas. And it's hard enough keeping things straight for myself and for Mom as it is; I have no wish to complicate our relationship any further by saying or suggesting things that she might retain and then fixate upon.

Every now and then, Mom comes to me and says she wants to go back to Florida. Yesterday, I told her in no uncertain terms that I am not willing to go with her, and the next trip I take is going to be a *real* vacation. Bob and I haven't gone anywhere (with the exception of a few long weekends) for ourselves since 2005. All our other travels have revolved around helping her. This October is our twentieth wedding anniversary and we're going to Italy to celebrate for ten days or so.

Mom said she thought we had gone to San Francisco recently. I said no, that was 2005, more than five years ago. She said she could stay in Florida by herself, that she'd "manage" as she had before. I reminded her that the reason she's here is that she was *not* "managing."

And then, I pivoted. I simply told her that she's not a prisoner. I handed her the phone.

"Go ahead. Make some calls. Book your flight. Call for a limo to the airport. I won't stop you. If you're competent enough to arrange your own travels, you have my blessing."

She looked down at the floor and got quiet.

I don't want to be mean. And I don't want to lie to her. I want her to be as comfortable and happy as she's capable of being. But the last thing I want to do is take her back to Florida so she can be reunited with the inescapable fact that her life there is over and her future is in New Jersey with family and a network of caregivers. The truth is painful, but less so than facing the repeated dissolution of the fantasy to which she keeps returning, that she is capable of living an independent life.

CHAPTER 14:
PAINLESS

March 17, 2011

The other day, Mom complained that she had a "toothache." She corrected herself and acknowledged that of course she didn't have any actual teeth, and so it was technically a "gum ache." Mom has a full denture plate on the top and a full set of implants on the bottom.

I asked her if she had cleaned her dentures lately and she admitted that she hadn't. I told her that her caregiver would be arriving soon and could help her with that task.

I was busy with a lot of other things, and when the caregiver arrived, I welcomed her, told her about Mom's discomfort and the need to attend to her oral hygiene. She acknowledged my request and I went back to work.

A little later, I noticed Mom nodding on the sofa in the living room. I went over, put a hand on her arm and asked her if she felt all right. She looked up at me and grinned blissfully. "I found my pills."

"You took painkillers?"

"Yeah. I feel great."

"You took Vicodin rather than clean your teeth."

"Sure."

"When it wears off, you're going to have pain again."

"I'll take more pills."

When I told my husband this story later that evening, he laughed, acknowledging that he probably shouldn't be laughing at this. What the hell. It's pretty funny. It's also kind of scary. I'm going to have to search her room for her stash.

Today (Thursday) Mom was on a treasure hunt in the fridge. My brother had brought a load of smoked fish and bagels on Sunday. (This is one of the few joys my brother and mother share. I hate fish. No one else in my brother's household eats it either.) I had sliced the many leftover bagels and frozen them in a plastic bag, sliced up the chocolate babka he'd brought (watch *Seinfeld* for details) and put it in a plastic bag so she could grab slices as she pleased, and put all the other various leftovers in the refrigerator.

Somewhere along the line in one of her feeding frenzies, Mom had put all the stuff in the freezer and forgot about it. She was searching through the refrigerator for so long this afternoon, the door alarm was ringing as her caregiver looked on, helplessly. I came over and Mom asked me what I did with her food. I hadn't touched it. I looked around and then looked in the freezer. Everything was there. I told her she had to have put it there. "Put me in front of a firing squad!" she exclaimed dramatically.

"Mom, you're the one who did this and you're the only one who cares. So if there's a firing squad involved, you're going to have to hire them to shoot you."

I got an excellent offer on Mom's apartment in Florida this week. I plan to use the proceeds to move her to an assisted living place up here. This is the best day I've had in a long time. There's light at the end of the tunnel, and these "funny" incidents will seem a whole lot funnier in retrospect, several years from now, when the pain has faded from my memory.

CHAPTER 15:
VIEW OF
THE FALLS

March 27, 2011

At the end of February, on a Monday morning, I heard noises coming from Mom's room. I knocked and opened her door to find her sitting on the floor with her legs splayed open and a large purple knot on her left leg. It looked like her knee might be dislocated. She said she needed to go to the bathroom and couldn't get up.

"Mom, why didn't you call for us?"

"I didn't want to bother you."

Bob helped slide her across the varnished hardwood floor down the hall and to the bathroom. She giggled as they went. I called 911, and the police and paramedics came quickly. They were very kind and took her to the closest hospital. I followed in my car and took care of the administrative stuff.

At the hospital, I learned that Mom had been sitting there on the floor in her room for hours. She had fallen in the middle of the night and I hadn't heard it. The noise we did hear was Mom trying to pull herself up on the bed as it slid across the floor. She had bumped her head. The lump on her leg was a hematoma. After lots of tests, she was pronounced merely bruised and was cleared to go home.

In the days that followed, we iced her leg and she came around. Her leg turned purple and healed.

Yesterday, Bob and I went to capture video of our town's St. Patrick's Day Parade. There were many marching bands, emergency vehicles from all over the area, scouts, sports teams, and vintage cars. It was a cool, clear, sunny Saturday and everyone had a ball. I run my town's public access TV station and this is one of my jobs, one I really enjoy.

I hadn't hired a caregiver for the day. I hoped Mom would be okay on her own for a couple of hours.

Bob and I went for a quick bite at a local restaurant after the parade and then headed home. As I ascended the stairs, my older cat, Max, was poised at the top in a posture I hadn't seen before, and our new cat, Cody, was at his side. They both looked at me as if to say, "'bout time you got here, Mom!" I noticed my mother's slippers splayed on the dining room floor near her makeup bag.

I called to my mother and went to her room. She was sitting on her bed with tissues wadded in a knee-high sock to staunch the bleeding from her right knee. She'd fallen again, this time apparently tripping on the dining room area rug on her way out of the kitchen, where she had been applying makeup. She told me that when she opened her eyes, Max was standing over her, looking concerned. The two cats sat by her as she tried to figure out how to get herself up.

I cleaned her wound, dressed it with gauze and an Ace bandage, and called to Bob. I gave her some acetaminophen for the pain. I helped her put on elastic-waist pants and sneakers. We were off to the ER again.

We stayed with Mom as they examined, monitored, CAT-scanned, and X-rayed her. A man in a nearby room was resuscitated and shocked back to life several times as they played the theme from *ER* over the PA system (no joke!). It was pretty intense. We were there more than five hours waiting for Mom to be released.

We got home around 11 p.m. I fed Mom, gave her ibuprofen, and got her to bed. Bob and I watched a movie, had a bite, and went to bed ourselves.

Today, I finally got around to opening the mail from Friday. Mom's health insurance carrier denied her claim for X-rays from the February fall because they said her auto insurance should be the primary insurer in this case. So tomorrow, before taking her to her podiatrist, I have to call the imbeciles at Mom's Medicare Advantage plan and explain that Mom's injuries had nothing to do with a car accident and try to get them on the correct page with the new claim coming their way from yesterday's misadventure.

I have appointments with three assisted living facilities in the coming week and I will be contacting her long-term care provider to change the benefit from in-home to residential. I need to get her situated before I leave for Florida at the end of April to clean out her apartment and close on its sale. Then I can go without worrying about caregiver schedules and all that nonsense. She needs to be monitored all the time. That has become abundantly clear.

And I'll have to get her to her regular geriatric doctor for a follow-up soon too. I am also in the market for a good cloning facility so I can assign some of this to another me.

Good Lord, I am so due for a vacation.

CHAPTER 16:
SWEET RELIEF

April 1, 2011

I spent the entire week looking for, finding, and signing up to get Mom situated in an assisted living apartment. When I walked into one particular facility in Wayne, the place was clearly different. The residents looked alive and happy. The staff came across as caring in a genuine way. And I told them food was important, so they sent me home with meals for Mom and me, and she loved them.

They had a one-bedroom available for immediate occupancy and they gave me a deal on the first month at a studio "respite rate" with no community fee. Mom's long-term care will pick up part of it, and when she becomes a "resident," they pick up even more of the cost.

The day after I went on my tour, Mom had her appointment with her doctor to follow up on her injuries from her fall last week. He told us she needed physical therapy. I asked him if we could speak privately. I told him my plans and that she could have the needed therapy at her new home. He thought it was a great idea and he promptly filled out the paperwork and gave me what I needed to get her enrolled. His associate makes house calls there regularly, too, so there will be continuity in her healthcare.

I resolved to tell her today, Friday, and steeled myself for the worst. As I had hoped, she was actually glad, and was looking forward to being in a more social setting. I told her about the physical therapy and how she's resistant here, but would be more inclined to do the work in a more professional setting. She agreed and told me she's been feeling guilty about interfering with our lives to such a high degree. I just smiled.

Well, I've got to go pack up her room. Tomorrow, we get the truck, empty the storage locker[5] and bring most of her stuff to her new apartment. It'll be a lot of work, but this is the last big push. Monday, I bring her in, get her settled and start my own life anew. I can't believe it's almost here.

---

[5] In order to hold onto Mom's various furniture pieces and cherished items, I rented a storage locker. When you don't know where someone might ultimately land as their needs change, these facilities can save you a lot of aggravation.

CHAPTER 17:
FAREWELL
TO FLORIDA

May 4, 2011

I grew up in a household where money was always tight. One time, when I was about twelve, I remember needing shoes for a school performance, and when I asked my father for money to buy them, he freaked out and said he was going to leave home. I vowed never to ask him for money again.

I moved out of the family home in 1978, when I graduated from college at the tender age of twenty. About ten minutes after I left, my father started making money in the bar business. He finally found the right location and started earning a great living.

In 1984 Dad landed in the hospital for coronary bypass surgery. He was fifty-six, an obese heavy smoker and drinker. Installation of a "zipper" in his chest persuaded him to give up the cigarettes and go easy on the booze. He couldn't quite give up the overeating or embrace physical fitness, but he did the best he could.

Dad also realized he had a second chance to be a better husband to his wife, and to let loose and spend some of the assets he had acquired. I had gone to school on scholarship, and my brother didn't care much for college, so we didn't incur any educational debt to weigh them down. They felt

44

free to spend their discretionary dollars on all kinds of stuff for themselves.

In the late '80s, my parents bought two properties: a three-bedroom house on Barnegat Bay in south Jersey and a two-bedroom co-op on the Intracoastal Waterway in southeast Florida. They sold their house in Brooklyn and split their time between New Jersey and Florida. Eventually, the "snowbird" life became a little too much, as they preferred to spend more of their time in the tropical weather. They sold the house in south Jersey and went full time in Florida.

The combined detritus they acquired through the years wound up in the five capacious closets of their Florida co-op. They filled every available cubic inch with stuff, from clothes and shoes to tools, electronics, bric-a-brac, and "artwork." They didn't throw or give anything away. They didn't have to. They had storage space and a Depression-era mentality that said "keep it just in case."

When Dad died, Mom reluctantly gave his clothes to charity. But she gradually took over his huge clothes closet and filled it with more clothing and shoes of her own. Her weekly jaunts to T.J. Maxx provided her with entertainment and the joy of finding sandals for twenty-three cents, in five different colors.

Mom's girlfriends in the building found her shopping habits rather astonishing. One friend of Mom's told me she had advised her to start paring down her belongings so as not to leave the chore to her kids. I wish she had taken that advice.

So last week, I had the incredible good fortune of finding a buyer for their apartment after one day on the market. They even bought the furniture. But they certainly didn't want all the *stuff*. The overwhelming task fell to, you guessed it, her child.

Wait a minute, Tracey. You have a brother, don't you? Yes, I do. And when I told him of the sale, and the great price, and the quickness of the closing, he was mightily impressed and insisted on coming down to help. He knew what was involved. He'd seen the inside of those stuffed caverns for himself. "Overwhelming" is an understatement.

I also have a husband. And by coincidence, he was asked to play a gig with a band on April 30, right around the proposed closing date. He would come down to help, but he would have to leave on Wednesday.

Problems arose as the closing date drew near. The mortgage on the apartment had to be settled.

Settled? Dad had told me that the mortgage had been paid off years ago. Unfortunately, this was never recorded with the county on the deed. I had to find the proof of the loan's satisfaction. The realtor had checked my parents' file cabinet for me, but found nothing. I had a hunch and a key to a safe deposit box. I was flying down Monday afternoon. The closing was Friday afternoon.

The Friday before, I hadn't heard from my brother so I sent him a text message. I told him we were taking Mom out for lunch on Easter Sunday and he was welcome to join us. And would we be seeing him in Florida next week?

In a word, "*No.*" He hemmed and hawed and texted me that he had to be in Guatemala on Monday. Then Nicaragua. Maybe he could come via Mexico City next Saturday (the day after the closing).

I told him I'd handle it.

Bob and I flew down and went straight to the apartment. I checked all the files for the document we needed. Nada. Then I went to the big leatherette accordion portfolio full of crap in the closet. Grandparent death certificates. Mom's elementary school graduation diploma. Receipts for their *objets d'art.* Formica samples from a long-ago kitchen renovation. And then, finally, "Satisfaction of Mortgage" documents from 1991. Hooray! Let's get hammered! (I found out a couple of days later that the safe deposit box key in my possession was for a box my mother had closed out in 2005.)

I had decided not to stay in the apartment. It was dusty and depressing, and I wanted someone to feed and clean up after me. So I got a great deal on a stay at a nearby deluxe hotel. We had room service the first night and rested up for the horrors to come.

The gal who runs the condo office was on vacation, and the woman who filled in for her was a tenant who knew a little about how to get things done. When I got into the apartment, I was confronted with a huge hole cut in the second bathroom wall. I had known they were doing work in the building, but I had been assured they would repair it. Four days until closing; I couldn't sell the place this way.

A maintenance man was sent to fix the hole. He did a splendid job. Bob and I told him to take any tools he wanted from my Dad's cache. The janitor came up and we told her she could take stuff too. Bless her, she took a lot and came back the next day for seconds.

We started clearing out the closets, drawers, and cabinets. Bob and I filled more than fifty black plastic trash bags with clothes, shoes, and household items. We loaded up the rented Grand Cherokee and brought the stuff to Goodwill. In the ensuing days, Bob made four more trips to the Goodwill store.

I donated Dad's computer, printer, and all the software, paper, and ink to a charity that trains veterans.

We had to pry the stereo equipment out of its cabinet. Something had spilled in there years ago and fused the components to the shelf.

I bubble-wrapped and boxed framed pictures and "tchotchkes" for Mom (and found the shawls she asked for and used them as filler too). I grabbed important papers and selected some tools and items that might be useful for us. I gathered old financial documents and boxed them for destruction.

Long before I put the apartment on the market, I had the contents evaluated by professional appraisers. I learned that while many of the items in question had given my parents a great deal of pleasure, they had very little market value. On their advice, I got in touch with the guy who sold the artwork to my folks to work a consignment deal. He came to the apartment, made me a cash offer for the pieces, took their Erté statue with him, and then reneged on his offer the next day. I retrieved the statue from him before leaving Florida and had it shipped to my home. I could do nothing about the wall hangings; they were simply too large. I hoped he would find buyers and do right by me, but I kept my expectations low.[6]

Wednesday afternoon, I had to take Bob to the airport. Wednesday evening, the cleaning guy I hired arrived with his helper. Lovely, hard-working people who spoke Portuguese, it took me a while to explain in fractured Spanish that they could take stuff for themselves. We threw a lot of stuff down

---

[6]   Two years later, I contacted the art dealer, asking that the two pieces be shipped to me. He said he had just moved to a new space and would look for them. Two weeks after that call, I got a check for the two pieces in the mail, for the amount stated on the consignment contract. The check cleared.

the trash chute. I worked past midnight with them. We made a great deal of headway.

Thursday morning, I arrived at the co-op parking lot to find a car parked illegally in my spot. I went to the office. The gal who runs the place was back from vacation, and after greeting me warmly, asked if I'd been throwing out garbage last night after 10 p.m. I said yes, and she told me I was going to be fined one hundred dollars. I said I'd write a check after she got my parking space vacated. She gave me the number of the towing company; I called them and they told me the office had to call them. So I called her, she called them, the tow truck was on the way. Don't you just love efficiency?

I had to get my mother's huge treadmill out of the bedroom. A guy had come to see it the night before and said he would come back for it. I called him and he said he'd call back. I called the office to check on another matter, mentioned the treadmill, and the office manager asked if she could have it. (Bob said I should have demanded one hundred dollars from her.) I said yes, she sent the maintenance guys, and an hour later, after taking doors off hinges and humping the thing hither and yon, the beast was removed from the apartment.

I brought the old financial documents to be shredded. Then I went to the spa at the resort for my massage. I finally got someone to take care of me. This wasn't a luxury; it was a necessity. And it was the best massage of my life so far. I slept pretty well that night.

Friday morning, I checked out of the hotel, filled the truck with gas, dealt with the statue (which I retrieved from the unscrupulous art dealer and shipped home), and then went back to the apartment for one last look around. Everything looked good. Then I opened the dishwasher.

In the basket, there was a load of old bottle brushes, spatulas, and assorted kitchen crap. I took it to the chute. Looking through the pieces, I did find one treasure: a steel jar opener that is no longer manufactured. It still works. I had always wanted it. Now it is mine.

The walk-through and closing went fine. I got kudos from the attorneys and realtors on locating the Satisfaction of Mortgage document and walked out with a great big check. I deposited it in Mom's account on the way to the airport.

My flight was delayed about forty-five minutes, but I had a nice meal at the airport while I waited and decompressed. We landed about fifteen minutes late and Bob was there to meet me.

The icing on this cake was my brother's response. Clearly afraid to talk to me, he sent texts. While I was cleaning the apartment on Wednesday night: "How's it going?" My reply: "Still cleaning." "Sorry!" Oh, how helpful.

Saturday, another text: "How'd it go? Just got home." My reply: "*Done.*"

Rather than try to deal with this as a text dialogue, I sent him a letter. He hates my letters. They make him read. They make him think. And he can't just fire back with an easy "reply."

"Going forward, I will take care of Mom's expenses and health care. Visit her regularly. When the boxes arrive from Florida, help her deal with the contents.

"When she dies, you will be responsible for dealing with the contents of her apartment.

"Sincerely,
Tracey"

He called me on the way home from work Tuesday night.

"How'd it go?" I told him coldly it was a horror, that I didn't care to go into it, but it was done. We closed. Money's in the bank.

How was Guatemala? He said it didn't go well.

"Have you spoken to Mom?" Saw her today. "How is she?" Seems fine.

Then he got home and saw my letter. He replied with an email.[7] It was absolutely hateful. No one twisted my arm to be Mom's caregiver. He accused me of taking on Mom's care for the money and framed me as being unreasonable for not being willing to change the closing date to accommodate his schedule, as if I had any control over this aspect of the deal. The buyer wanted this. I wasn't going to jeopardize the sale to a bona fide buyer.

He screws up, but it's somehow my fault. How dare I make him feel so guilty (without even trying)? Don't I understand that his crushing guilt should be punishment enough? He had a once-in-a-lifetime opportunity that went nowhere, but he had to do it! He has a family. I don't. Just stupid cats. How dare I?

That's gratitude for you.

Farewell to Florida. Farewell to my brother. May karma work its wonders as I move forward and start taking better care of my husband, my cats, and myself. And no one's twisting my arm.

---

7   Author's note: In my original blog, I quoted my brother's email verbatim. Since my mother's passing, my brother and I have come to a better place in our relationship. I do not wish to upset the delicate balance we've managed to find, so I have elected to summarize and paraphrase. Every family has their own version of these kinds of clashes, so I think it's important to acknowledge ours. I love my brother and I'm glad we've been able to move on. No doubt this positive turn of events would please our parents.

CHAPTER 18:
JEWISH MAFIA

May 22, 2011

I called Mom on Monday morning to see how she was doing. She said she was fine, but she's been waiting for a call to go to the meeting where she would see her husband again. They found him. My brother and sister-in-law know all about it.

She is now convinced that a man in a wheelchair living at her residence is her "ex." He doesn't want to talk to her and she wants to know what she's done to upset him. He was a connected guy, and the Jewish Mafia has brought him back.

Later, Mom called me while I was on the phone with a client. She was very upset. She might have to file a complaint and have him arrested. Maybe she'll call for a cab and go to her apartment. She tells me I'm making her feel like an idiot. I'm actually not saying anything, I'm just listening quietly and getting pretty bent out of shape myself.

She wants me to call my brother. I told her to hang in there and I'd try to get some answers.

The business manager at Mom's home answered the phone. I was glad to hear her voice; she's a very nice, kind person. She asked me what was up. I said, "My mother's freaking me out." She said that was not uncommon and she would connect me to "Wellness."

The head nurse, another person I'd come to know and trust, picked up. I asked her if she'd heard anything about my mother being particularly weird. She said no. I told her that Mom is convinced that her dead husband is now living there and I'm afraid she might be harassing some poor, unsuspecting resident in a wheelchair. Then she recalled that she *had* heard something. They were in fact going to collect a urine specimen to see if perhaps a urinary tract infection (UTI) was responsible.

I started researching the web and decided to call my mom's doctor. They have an associate who pays house calls at the home. The doctor called me back on Tuesday and I told her about Mom's sudden agitation and profound delusions. She said she would arrange for a battery of tests at the hospital.

After calling Mom's insurance company and getting a royal runaround, I spoke to the doctor again and she assured me that taking Mom to the ER was fine; when a patient goes suddenly acutely wacky, it's time-sensitive and the hospital would navigate the insurance for me. I went to get Mom.

She was dressed and waiting for me in the lobby. She seemed pretty calm. I kissed her and went up to Wellness for her paperwork. I glanced at her medication list. I didn't realize she'd been put on a new blood pressure medication. Good thing I looked!

After getting Mom into a heavier coat (she doesn't go out much, and it was a raw, nasty, rainy day), we were off to the hospital. She was much less agitated than on Monday and she talked about a lot of things, nothing too troubling.

When we got to the ER, I checked her in and Mom enjoyed watching the fish in the big tank in the waiting room from her comfy wheelchair. Eventually, we were called and screened by a nurse who asked what the problem was. I told her gently that my mother thought her dead husband was miraculously reconstituted. Mom pretended to close her ears when she saw my discomfort with reporting the issue in front of her. The nurse asked Mom if she knew where her husband was, and she replied, "In the Atlantic." This is true. We took Dad's ashes to his old boat slip on the Intracoastal below their apartment and committed them to the water on the first anniversary of his death.

So she knows he's dead, but there's this man at the home who looks like Dad to her, and she seems to realize it's in very large part a wish fulfillment fantasy. She believed it because she really wanted to.

Anyway, once she got situated in a room, we were interviewed by a lovely physician's assistant. They were going to run a lot of tests: blood, urine, chest X-ray, EEG, CAT scan of her head. I waited with her until 6:30. My husband came to wait with her to go for her CAT scan (everything else was done in the room) as I had to go to Borough Hall in Ringwood to air a council meeting at 8 p.m.

Mom did indeed have a urinary tract infection. They administered IV antibiotics and admitted her. When I called Wednesday morning she was really out of it. I spoke to her nurse about the antibiotic. They had given her Levaquin. I asked the nurse to get her off it ASAP. I had told them she reacted badly to Levaquin, but they put her on it anyway. The nurse said she'd see about getting her switched. I called the doctor to make sure. I was assured a different drug would be used.

The day after Mom was admitted, I received an *Aging Care* Newsletter featuring an article on UTIs in the elderly. While I had known that UTIs cause delusional symptoms, this article hit on everything: predisposing factors, complications, and much more. Reading the comments, I got a really good idea of just how prevalent this is. Makes you wonder how many people in dementia care facilities have this readily addressable (and potentially deadly) condition.

When I called the nurse on Thursday, she verified that the antibiotic was changed as soon as I asked. Mom sounded better over the phone.

Friday, I went to visit. I have no idea how long she will be in the hospital, but Mom's still mighty confused. She rambled on at length about a lot of things, but one thing that finally emerged was that she had been experiencing burning on urination and couldn't get anyone to help her. I told her she could always tell me. But now I know: I have to ask her specifically if she's having those problems. I asked her often when she lived with me as part of her regular "inventory" of complaints.

It's really hard for me to listen to her. She speaks at length about places and people, but when I try to understand what and who, she gets frustrated because she can't remember and can't put names to the things she pictures. The only thing that's clear to me is that she has really vivid dreams, and when she wakes, she has a tough time discerning what she dreamed from what's real. I suspect her TV watching gets thrown into the cauldron too.

I'm going to have to bring all this up at the next meeting of the Jewish Mafia. I need answers, damn it!

CHAPTER 19:
REHAB

May 27, 2011

Mom's stay at the hospital lasted several days. I was afraid she'd be discharged over the weekend. Her delusions were staying with her and she was in no condition to go back to the home. Her gout flared up on Sunday morning, making her left foot too sore to walk on. I diagnosed the problem over the phone as soon as the neurologist described it to me, but it took until late Sunday afternoon to get her anti-inflammatory prescribed. I resisted the temptation to bring her medication with me. (I still have all her drugs in the rolling cart I bought for her in my kitchen.) That delayed her release another day, and that turned out to be a good thing. The hospital's social workers are only in during the week, not on weekends. This gave me time to make sure Mom would be transferred to a rehab facility to get stronger and hopefully, somewhat grounded in a more widely accepted version of "reality."

After a few calls on Monday, the hospital arranged to have Mom transported to Wanaque Care Center for rehabilitation treatment. They are "in network" for her insurance and pretty close to my home. I asked the social worker what she knew about the place and she assured me she'd heard "good things."

Tuesday morning, I went to Mom's home (the assisted living facility or "ALF" where she'd been living) to pack a bag for her. I was told to bring a week's worth of clothes. I packed extra underwear, Poise pads, toothbrush and toothpaste, hair brushes, moisturizer, makeup, slippers, shoes, nightgown, blouses, slacks, and a hoodie. I also spoke to one of the staff members at the ALF who filled in some of the details about the days leading up to Mom's hospitalization. She had indeed shared her suspicions about her dead husband living at the home and this was noted as an abrupt change in a previously delightful resident.

When I got to the rehab center, I gave Mom's suitcase to the receptionist for labeling (they label all the contents with the patient's name). I was sent to the third floor to see Mom.

Mom's roommate is lucid and seems nice. She loves to look out the window at the view of a mountain. She told me Mom was in therapy. I asked at the desk and was told she was in the dining room. Sure enough, she was in a wheel-chair, dressed in a blue scrub top and brown velour pants (not hers; these were loaners meant to tide her over until her own clothes arrived).

Clearly glad to see me, Mom asked me to wheel her to a different part of the room. She wanted to get away from the AC vents.

Her mind wasn't any clearer. Now, her dead husband is "a broad." Yes, that's right, Dad is now a transsexual woman. When she pointed her out to me, I simply said, "No, Ma." She smiled and said, "Not buying it, huh?" I could only smile and shake my head.

A social worker from the rehab center had phoned me while I was en route to the facility to give me a status update. Now she came over to join us. A nice Jewish lady with eastern European roots, she conversed easily with Mom, sprinkling her language with some choice Yiddish expressions.

I mentioned the delusions to her, and she said, yes, a UTI will do that. Yeah, but will she be coming down from orbit anytime soon?

I left Mom eating lunch and told her I'd be back. She wanted to come home with me. I told her gently that she'd be there a few days to get stronger so she could go back to her apartment.

Downstairs, I met with the director of the place to fill out paperwork; pretty straightforward, but lots of it. They'd exercise her, get a psychiatrist to chat with her, feed her, dispense her meds, do her laundry, even cut and style her hair (I gave them some money to doll her up). Her primary doctor is on the board of the place, and they are developing a relationship with Mom's ALF, too, so I'm hoping for a well-coordinated effort to transition Mom back to assisted living.

So now, we wait. A few days of evaluations and therapy, followed by conferences with the folks at the home to see if she's ready to go back. Meanwhile, I'll visit her and make sure she's getting the care she needs.

I thought this was supposed to get easier. Not having to be hands-on with her daily certainly is. Still, I can't help but think that maybe if she'd have been with me, I'd have noticed the UTI sooner. Maybe not. At least I'm not flying down to Florida to deal with this. Yeah, that's it, the bright side!

CHAPTER 20:
GERIATRIC DELINQUENT

May 31, 2011

"I was so proud of myself!" Mom beamed as she recalled defending herself from the evil conspirators with a butter knife. Safe, calm, and cheerful in her bed at the Chilton ER, her home away from home, she rambled amiably about the adventure that led to the police removing her from the rehab center that Sunday.

We had visited Mom at the rehab on Friday of Memorial Day weekend. She was using an "ambi-walker," which afforded her the ability to walk with wheeled support and sit when she got unsteady or tired. She'd been receiving physical therapy. She had been bathed, her hair washed and combed. "I love this ship!" Mom gushed. "It's amazing."

Saturday I'd been called to approve the use of a bracelet on Mom that would prevent the elevator from moving when she got on it. Now ambulatory, Mom was ambulating and looking for adventure. Mostly, she wanted a cab to take her home, wherever that was.

Seemingly happy and improving physically, Bob and I left her Friday afternoon to enjoy the rest of the long weekend. On Saturday, we lunched at Greenwood Lake, went over to our sailboat, did some cleanup, and prepped for sailing the next day. Saturday night, we had reservations at the Blue Note in Manhattan to see Stanley Clarke. Traveling into town on the holiday weekend was a breeze. I even found street parking less than two blocks from the club. We enjoyed the show immensely and had a lovely evening.

Sunday, our niece arrived with her boyfriend. We took them out on the boat and had a really nice time. The weather was beautiful: hot, sunny, and breezy. We had a little trouble with our jib (the sail at the front of the boat) and couldn't get the furler to retract it. I worked on it for a good long while and we had to drop the sail. We made it back to the marina, and just as we were tying up, my phone rang. "Your mother is threatening staff and other residents with cutlery. Can you please come here and try to calm her down?" I told them I'd get there as quickly as I could.

We finished closing the boat, dropped some stuff off at the house and headed to the rehab center. On the way, my phone rang again. "We had to call the police. They're bringing her to Chilton ER."

Huh boy. We headed over to the hospital where the staff was just starting on her. We waited outside her room while they changed her into hospital garb and ran a few tests.

"Okay, Slash. What happened?"

Mom reported calmly that they were all in cahoots. They were going to steal the boat and she was going to tell on them. That one who was her best friend turned out to be the ringleader. But she showed her. They came after her with a sword, but she grabbed up all the knives and defended herself. She giggled as she recalled the incident. She defended herself! She wasn't going to let them marry her off to that defective guy!

A nice young doctor came in and asked Mom why she was there. She tried but couldn't tell him. I gave him the broad strokes. He smiled and thanked me. We spoke outside.

He told me they'd repeat some of the tests to clear her medically and then she'd probably be transferred to Ramapo Ridge Psychiatric Hospital. The rehab center wouldn't take her back until she had forty-eight hours of psychiatric observation. She would be seen by a social worker who was on the way.

Bob took the kids back to the house; they were sweet about visiting Mom, but they didn't need to be subjected to all this. He got the barbecue grill and the hot tub going for them. He called me and said he'd come back and leave them to enjoy our little oasis on their own.

Meanwhile, the social worker came and talked to Mom and me. I filled in what Mom couldn't quite articulate and she agreed that Ramapo Ridge was the next stop. But I would have to sign papers to have her admitted and they'd need the hard copies of my power of attorney and health care proxy. Could I come back with them tomorrow morning?

We headed home around 9 p.m., knowing Mom was in good hands for the night. I dropped into the tub and spent time with the kids. I would have loved to have had a cocktail or three, but aside from the calories, getting up early with a hangover seemed like a bad idea.

I got up at 8, made coffee, ate breakfast, tended to the cats and my morning work items. I left for Chilton at 9 with the legal documents.

Back at the hospital, the gal I was supposed to see was on the phone. I went to see Mom. She was cozy in her bed watching TV. She couldn't see it though, because she didn't have her glasses. She said something about them being smashed. I called the rehab center; they had them, and they were intact. I could pick them up anytime.

The social worker came by and greeted me. She took the legal documents and sent them to Ramapo Ridge. She brought back forms for me to sign. I had to describe why Mom needed to go there and essentially commit her.

I helped Mom go to the bathroom a bunch of times and was impressed by how much better she was doing physically. She climbed in and out of bed deftly and was pretty steady on her feet. Recollections of her butter knife fight made her giddy.

By noon, we were still waiting to transfer Mom, so I asked if I could go and come back when they needed me. No problem. I got home in time to say goodbye to the kids. I had some lunch, did some work, and waited for the call.

Around 2:45, it came. "The doctor needs to talk to you." Oh?

On the way back to the hospital, we stopped at rehab for Mom's glasses and I grabbed a clean pair of jeans, a blouse, bra, and panties.

Back at the ER, I saw Mom's nurse. "I'm sorry. These insurance problems are tough."

Huh?

The social worker and the psychiatrist found me. They were ready to transfer her to Ramapo Ridge when they learned that they were out-of-network for Mom's insurance. Oh crap, what now?

Holy Name in Teaneck is in-network. Twice the distance, but that'll work.

Next problem: Holy Name needs Wanaque to sign a form that says they'll take her back after forty-eight hours before they'll admit her. It's a holiday, so there's no administrator to sign off.

I called the rehab center, told them it was an emergency, and got the big boss, who just happened to be visiting, on the phone. She said she'd be happy to sign off. Hooray!

Two hours of phone tag and misplaced faxes later, it was time to arrange an ambulance to transfer Mom to the psychiatric hospital. They'd be there in twenty minutes.

Meanwhile, I asked the nurse if during the nearly twenty-four hours Mom had been there she'd gotten any of her meds. Uhhh…

Nope. She hadn't. I went through the list with her, showed her what should have been dispensed. She ordered the pills and got her up to date for the day. And she sent the information on to Holy Name so they'd be ready for her.

After more confusion, the ambulance finally arrived. Mom greeted the EMTs warmly, certain she knew them. They put her on the gurney, and we followed them out to the waiting vehicle with Mom's personal effects.

We waved goodbye as they loaded her on the ambulance and closed the doors. The Memorial Day weekend was ending and we were finally heading home. And Mom was off to the psychiatric hospital. Do we know how to party or what?

CHAPTER 21:
METAPHORICALLY THINKING

June 14, 2011

Since this phase of Mom's life has unfolded, the psych major[8] in me can't help but find some fascination in her condition. Often, when Mom can't find words for what she wants to convey, she speaks in metaphors. Boats loom large in her metaphorical lexicon. When she first got to rehab, she was very happy and thought she was on a cruise ship. Later, when her paranoia was in full swing, the thieves were trying to steal her boat.

Before her dementia became evident, another metaphorical term was established: "Home." Shortly after my father's death in 2004, all my mother wanted was to go home. Florida. Hallandale. Her apartment. She had been living in assisted living in New Jersey with Dad. She stayed with Bob and me after Dad passed away. She campaigned to go home constantly. I arranged my schedule so I could take her back.

On the appointed day, I flew down with her to Fort Lauderdale, schlepped her luggage, picked up the rental car, and drove her to her place. As we approached her block, I

---

8   I have a BA with Honors in Psychology from NYU.

told her to smile, she got her wish. She was home. She drew a breath and sobbed, "I'm in hell."

Resisting the impulse to punch her, I took a deep breath. I had jumped through all these hoops to get her back to her beloved apartment, her home. But it finally sunk in: she didn't want to just go back to her place, she wanted to go back in time, to the life she used to have. "Home" was a metaphor for the life she had loved but could not reclaim.

Late last week, once Mom returned to the psychiatric hospital, my brother went to see her. She was glad to be there; it was better than the rehab center (which had gone from cruise ship to den of thieves in a matter of days). She asked my brother if he was going to see Dad while he was there.

"Dad's *here*?" he asked.

"Who do you think is driving the ship?" Mom replied. This little exchange had me giggling for the next couple of days. It made me feel that Mom was okay for the time being. If she thought Herby was steering, she felt like she was in good hands.

Bob and I went away for the weekend: a Saturday night concert in Asbury Park, a hotel stay in Lakewood, followed by a dolphin-watching cruise out of Atlantic City on Sunday. Just another little respite for the chronic caregiver.

I called the hospital on Monday to see how Mom was doing. They were glad I called. Mom had wanted to speak to me over the weekend and they had called my home number rather than my cell. (How many times does one have to clarify contact information?!) The nurse taking care of Mom said she was "doing great" and they thought she might be released mid-week. The psychiatrist confirmed this prognosis.

Then I spoke to the nurse from the assisted living facility (Mom's last "permanent" address) who had gone to evaluate

Mom that morning. She found her to be profoundly confused. Mom told her that I had been in an accident and was in a coma. The nurse assured her she had spoken to me recently and I was fine. Mom insisted it had just happened. I thanked her for the information and asked if she thought Mom had a chance of returning to assisted living. Her response: "I'd like to see her a lot more stable."

I went to visit Mom so she could see I was okay. I got caught in a huge traffic jam and arrived after visiting hours, but was permitted to see her anyway. When I got to the floor, Mom was in a group session. She lit up when she saw me. Going by the comments I heard from her cohorts, Mom had been crying and upset that her "sister" was critically injured. I introduced myself as her daughter, Tracey, and let one and all know I was quite all right, despite the hour sitting in traffic.

We went to Mom's room to chat. She had been collecting items in little plastic baskets. I looked around to see if they'd given her any of the clothes and personal effects I'd brought her. I couldn't find much in the room. She remarked that she didn't even have a tube of lipstick.

I went to the nurse's station and asked about her stuff. They kept her suitcase locked up in a hall closet. Could she have her makeup? She couldn't keep it in her room, but she certainly could use it when supervised. I handed Mom's cosmetic bag to her and she smiled broadly.

"That's what I meant to pack!"

"Okay, good. You can have this whenever you want it, Mom. It's yours. Just ask the nurses."

She fished out a tube of lipstick and put it on without a mirror. She brightened. She picked a bright fuchsia color, which complemented her tie-dyed T-shirt.[9]

Her confusion was obvious, but she was calmer. Her thoughts were cloudier than usual. This is doing great?

Today, I called the Alzheimer's Hot Line, a resource for families affected by dementia. The woman I spoke with listened patiently and sympathetically. She heard my concerns and frustrations. She recommended I reach out to the caseworker at the hospital to see if we could talk about Mom's next steps. Maybe she and/or Mom's doctor could recommend an appropriate "Plan B" facility in case she could not go back to the place she last lived.

I called the caseworker at the psychiatric hospital and voiced my concerns. She said she had spoken with the doctor this morning and he was still looking at releasing her midweek (today is Tuesday!). I asked where they proposed to send her and if they felt she was stable enough to return to assisted living. She said they would coordinate with Mom's facility. She also said that there was another facility I might consider, and it was adjacent to Mom's current residence. They take only memory-impaired patients, many with psychiatric issues.

Speaking with the referred facility, they sounded appropriate, but they don't accept Medicaid. That means that when the money runs out, Mom would have to move again. So Mom's current residence is the better choice. I'll just have

---

[9]   Mom acquired lots of odd clothing in her travels. The transient nature of people in these facilities means a lot of stuff gets misplaced, left behind and changes hands. Which also accounts, at least in part, for the appearance of things being "stolen."

to talk to them about moving Mom to the "memory wing" of the building and the associated costs.

As I was writing, Mom called me. She's upset. There's trouble. Mike was shot. Who's Mike, Mom? "My husband to be." He's dead. She saw him. They don't want to keep him in a casket. She's exhausted, her back hurts, and her mouth keeps sticking together. Okay, Mom. I'm going to call the desk and ask them to help you.

I called the nurse's station and told them my mother was in full-blown delusional mode, that she believes a man was shot and killed, that she needed some water, and probably needed to lie down for a while. I was thanked for the heads-up on Mom's condition and assured they would act on it.

I suppose it is possible that "Mike" being shot is a metaphor for the death of this particular delusion, but I wouldn't bet the ranch on it.

How can a woman who is so clearly in distress be defined as "doing great," on track for imminent release? What kind of metaphor could be applied here? Kicking the can down the road seems apt. But if I have anything to say about it, that can isn't getting kicked anywhere until I know it will land safely on a comfortable shelf.

CHAPTER 22:
A PLACE TO CRASH

June 24, 2011

It seemed like Mom was doing okay on Seroquel, an antipsychotic drug. She was calmer. The delusions were very much with her, but she wasn't "acting out." At least until Sunday.

A call came from the psychiatric hospital. Mom had fallen in the kitchen and hit her head. They did a CAT scan, and she was fine.

Monday, I visited and found out *why* she fell. Mom was upset with her favorite nurse for attending to another patient, so she grabbed a package of crackers from a cabinet. She threw it at the nurse, lost her balance, and fell. Acting out. Again.

Mom's psychiatrist showed up. He changed her medication to Risperdal, another antipsychotic medication Dad had been given. They would keep her for a few more days and see how she responds.

Mom looked good. She had color in her cheeks. She was happy to see me. She wanted to tip her favorite crew member (nurse). She had good energy, but she did have pain on her left side.[10] She'd been tested thoroughly and they could find no reason for it, so acetaminophen was prescribed.

When I got home, I decided to research Mom's psychiatric medications. At the top of the Risperdal page, a huge scary warning was posted saying this medication was extremely dangerous for elderly patients with dementia. *What?*

Further research revealed that *all* drugs of this type are dangerous for people like Mom, but they are *all* that's available. That's why she needed to be monitored in the hospital. If she had a bad reaction, they could treat her on the spot.

I braced myself for another week at the psych hospital. When I called on Thursday to check her status, the caseworker picked up the phone and gave me the news: the nurse from Mom's assisted living facility and Mom's shrink had seen her that morning and agreed she could return to her apartment. Deep breath. Really?! Thank you!

Later that morning, the nurse from Mom's ALF called me directly and confirmed the decision. She cautioned that Mom was still clearly delusional. I told her I didn't expect that to improve and was prepared to discuss moving Mom to the "memory wing." Meanwhile, we'd see if being surrounded by familiar objects might stabilize her. Socializing with less disturbed people might also help.

I had to see clients that day, but I could carve out about an hour between appointments. I headed over to the ALF and went right up to Mom's apartment. She was sitting in the club chair in her living room, staring like a deer caught in the headlights.

---

[10] The pain on Mom's left side was likely caused by an undiagnosed condition called Polycythemia Vera, a very rare condition that typically afflicts men.

"Hey, Mom. How are you feeling?"

Her eyes met mine with no expression.

"Mom, it's me, it's Tracey. Are you okay?"

"Is Dad waiting in the car?"

"No, Mom."

"He's got a sixteen-year-old-now, you know."

"Mom, Dad doesn't have anything. He's dead."

She told me she was tired and very thirsty. I got her a bottle of cold water and poured her a glass. She wanted a housecoat and I got one out for her. I helped her change, hung up her clothes, and helped her to bed. I told her I had to go, but someone would be up in an hour or so to check on her and bring her to dinner.

"Next time, don't pull any tricks on me, okay?"

"I didn't pull any tricks, Mom. Mother Nature and that bitch, Old Age, have been doing all this."

She looked at me and seemed to recognize the truth of my words. I kissed her cheek and she snuggled into her comfy bed for a nice, soft landing. I left for my appointment, concerned but hopeful. What tricks does Mother Nature have in store for us next?

CHAPTER 23:
NEXT!

July 8, 2011

Mom seemed to be settling in back at her ALF. She was going down to the dining hall for her meals, dressing herself and trying to put on makeup. When we went to see her that Saturday, her outfit was a little bolder than what she generally wore: cleavage-revealing long blouse over Lycra leggings and topped with a denim jacket. Hmm.

Seated in the dining room and finishing up her dinner, we chatted with Mom and her dinner companion, a very nice lady who was hard of hearing and a Yankees fan. Mom told us her "ex" had been involved with this poor woman too. He had since moved on to a sixteen-year-old! (Here we go again.)

"He spotted me as soon as I got back. He said, 'I knew you'd be here.'" She beamed at the recollection.

When she would move in a certain way or laugh, her left side still hurt.[11] She determined that she had surgery on that

---

[11] What I later learned was that Mom had Polycythemia Vera. The pain on her left side was most likely a symptom of this undiagnosed condition. Dementia makes it especially difficult to discern, because you never know when a complaint is truly physical or imagined. When it's unusual and doesn't show up on any of the standard tests, it takes a clinician who has experience with the condition to recognize it.

side and was still recovering. That explained why she had been away in the hospital.

We went to the community room upstairs where a movie was cued to be shown on the big TV. We chatted a while longer. We were near the Wellness office and I asked if Mom was being given anything for the pain in her left side. A nurse came over and brought her acetaminophen.

Bob and I had a date to meet friends for dinner. We bade Mom goodbye and went to our next stop.

I called Mom the next day, Sunday. I asked her how she liked the movie and she said it was pretty good. She recalled the basics. She'd had a nice breakfast. Okay. So far so good.

Monday, the call came. "Tracey, your mother tried to leave on her own. Twice. She needs to be watched around the clock. You have to hire one-on-one caregivers."

What about the "memory wing?" There were no beds available, but they would check at sister facilities.

Oh crap. I was given a contact for an agency with which the ALF works. Nineteen dollars/hour, twenty-four hours a day. Totally affordable if you're Warren Buffet. It would be 456 dollars a day until they could find a "live in," which would knock it down to 205 dollars a day. And that's in addition to being charged for a higher level of care from the ALF! And I still haven't been able to satisfy Mom's long-term care insurance company in order to get reimbursed for the care she's been getting at the ALF (intermittently) since April.

I dug out a note I'd scribbled a couple of weeks ago. The agent from the placement agency I used had recommended Potomac Group Homes. They're a facility that's strictly for Alzheimer's and dementia patients.

I called the gal who handles admissions. Their facility in Montville currently has only seven residents. This would be perfect for Mom. One of her triggers is being among groups of people talking without including her. Her immediate thought is "conspiracy." They're setting her up for something. And then she acts out.

In a small setting with few residents and constant attention, she would no doubt be more comfortable. The "holistic" approach they offer aims to limit medication and emphasize accommodating the resident's specific needs and desires. They don't take Medicaid, but they promise to help find the appropriate next facility for Mom when the time comes. I've got almost five years to worry about it. Average life expectancy for people with Mom's issues is about five years anyway. Meanwhile, I'd just be happy to get her to stay in one place for a few months without urgent phone calls for a change.

They've already assessed her, and Potomac is ready to bring Mom in. I just have to sign the papers and give them a check. And they're an all-inclusive facility. They charge one price (significantly lower than Mom's current ALF and other larger facilities) for all levels of service. It's a lovely place too. Very warm and homey, with special areas that accommodate people with Mom's kinds of issues.

So today, I'm off to sign papers, get some administrative concerns addressed, and set a move-in date. Then, I pack up her clothes and personal effects, set up her room for her, and arrange to have Mom moved to her new place. For two weeks, they don't want me to see her so they can help acclimate and stabilize her.

Then my niece will go to Mom's ALF apartment and take her beautiful bedroom set and other items she might need to set up her first apartment on her own. Poor kid is excited but feels bad about the circumstances. I told her to be happy. She's giving these lovely things a new home. Mom won't be needing them any longer; she's becoming a different person with very different needs. And I pray that the new place will serve those needs and others to come in the months that lay ahead.

CHAPTER 24:
PASTE ON A HAPPY FACE

July 12, 2011

Good news. The doctor who makes house calls at Potomac is in-network for Mom's insurance. She can move in on Monday. I can move her stuff in over the weekend.

On Saturday, Bob and I ran errands, I shopped for some items Mom would need at the new place and headed over to her apartment at the ALF.

Mom was there with her 24-7 caregiver. She was watching TV and enjoying herself. I told her she was going to be trying out a new place and I needed to pack some of her stuff. She asked about the accommodations and where her husband would be staying. "He'll stay where he always stays, Mom." That satisfied her.

I set about packing. I used her towels to wrap her framed photos and reused cartons that had held the towels to pack her photo albums and other breakable stuff. In an attempt to help, she brought me some kitchen items, including a tray and some tea towels with a half-eaten apple inside. (I found another half-eaten apple in one of her closets.) I quietly trashed the old fruit and asked Bob to start bringing the heavy stuff out to the car.

It was almost dinnertime and Mom's caregiver took her downstairs. I told them I'd find them when we were ready to leave.

I packed two small cases with shoes and clothes. The toiletries, hygiene items, pillows, and sheets could stay until Monday. I'd pack those once Mom was on her way to Potomac.

Mom was dining in the "memory wing" where she chatted happily with other residents about being from Brooklyn and how it differed from life on Uranus. (Okay, I made up the Uranus part.) I gave the caregiver a hug, thanked her for taking good care of my Mom, and told her I'd be happy to refer her. I gave Mom a kiss, told her I'd see her soon, and met Bob at the car.

We went to Potomac and schlepped the stuff up the stairs to Mom's room. She was now going to live in a single, dormitory-type room rather than a multiple-room apartment. No private bath; she could slip and fall. No phone or TV; she could no longer operate these. She would make do with a single bed, dresser, armoire, and shelves.

Bob couldn't bear it and went back to the car to wait. I unpacked the pictures and displayed them on the shelf above the bed. I hung her terry robe and pink hoodie on pegs under the shelf, placed her pink slippers by the foot of the bed. I arranged her shoes in the wardrobe and realized I'd forgotten hangers. But I found places for everything I'd brought and there was room for more. Hangers, toiletries, and some more clothing items would wait until Monday.

I introduced myself to the weekend staff and looked around. Nice quiet bunch. I saw one man who looked nothing like my father, but he seemed friendly, robust, and the type of guy my mother pasted "Herby" faces on. He'd likely do just fine.

On the way home, I asked Bob what troubled him. He felt bad for my mother. It's the end of the line.

I set up an ambulance to bring Mom to Potomac on Monday around 11 a.m. That way, I didn't have to answer a lot of questions; I could go to her apartment at the ALF and finish up packing without half-eaten apples. And she could get to her new place in time for lunch.

When I got to the ALF on Monday after Mom's departure, I heard from the staff that she had been in great spirits. I got to her apartment and, bless her heart, she had tried to pack. A box marked "Fragile" had all kinds of crap in it: costume jewelry, a bag of slips, the original appraisal of her diamond engagement ring. Nothing breakable. I chose some things she might actually use and threw them in a suitcase.

Going through the Potomac check list, I made sure I had all the required items. I put aside stuff I'd lent her for retrieval some other day. I got a trolley, loaded it up, picked up the last of Mom's mail (*People* magazine), and packed the car.

I had a dentist appointment at 2, so I stopped at a diner for lunch and then headed to my dentist. While in the chair, I got a picture text message from the director of the home. Holy crap. Mom had attached herself to the man I thought she would. The grin on her face said it all. I haven't seen her that happy in years.

That grin says it all. (Photo courtesy of "Julia Roberts")

Due to an administrative snafu, my dentist appointment took longer than expected and I didn't get to Potomac until 5:30. When I got there, Mom was poring over a binder, wearing big glasses (she had left hers behind at her previous residence). I asked her where she got the glasses. "From my husband." She nodded over toward the fellow in the picture I'd been sent. "He's Herby. Herbert. However you want me to say it. I have documented proof!"

Putting on her own glasses, which I had retrieved from her old place, she showed me the binder. It was information I had provided about her: contact numbers, insurance, doctors. Nothing about Herby. But she was sure.

Okay, Mom. I'm happy for you. You enjoy yourself and I'll go up to your room to unpack.

I schlepped the bags and cases up to her room and started unpacking. One of the ladies brought me a bookcase for Mom's photo albums. She said Mom fondly reminded her of a former resident and it would be nice to have someone lively there for a change.

As I made the bed, Mom appeared. She sat in a chair and asked, "Did you see what she did for me?"

"You like the pictures, Mom?"

Oh yes, she just *loved* the room. She said she cried tears of joy when she first saw it.

She chatted on about her wonderful day as I continued making the bed, hanging her clothes and putting everything away. The bus ride over was "magical" and "lucky." Her dinner was delicious. She loves everyone she's met. The house is beautiful (what, this one's not a boat?) and she doesn't ever want to leave.

Another gal came up to check on Mom. She moves so quickly! The gal charged with watching Mom was relieved to find her with me. I told her it was okay and I would help her back down when I was done.

Mom wanted to bring her wedding album down to share with the others. It's a big, heavy book and I offered to take it for her. She insisted on carrying it herself. That and her cane, which I'd also just brought. I went down the stairs with her. She dropped the book with a loud thud. Attendants ran to the stairs. "Just a book, not me!" said Mom, cheerfully. I picked up the book and handed it back to her once she got down to the landing. She scampered to the table and started describing the pictures to anyone who would look.

The wife of a male resident introduced herself. Mom was sure this male resident wanted to "get into her pants," but his wife assured me he has the mental capacity of an infant. "I figure Mom's about seventeen at this point." Mom grinned and agreed. "It's a great place to be."

As Mom showed off her pictures, I spoke with the wife. Her husband has been in this condition for some time. She told me she visits evenings after work and would I like to have dinner some evening? I'll take her up on that.

Meanwhile, I learned that Mom's new boyfriend does not have dementia. He's deaf and had been misdiagnosed with dementia because of his hearing deficiency. But he and his family are happy with his placement at Potomac, so he's stayed. He really seems to like Mom. And now he gets to be Mom's new honey. And that's sweet for everyone involved.

CHAPTER 25:
LOVE IN BLOOMERS

July 15, 2011

Maybe I am a genius after all. Maybe I just have great instincts. Or it could be dumb luck. (Lord knows I've been due for a little of that!) Whatever the case, Mom is really taking to her new surroundings and ingratiating herself to everyone at her new home.

The director of the facility told me how cute Mom and her new beau were together. He's profoundly deaf and he uses an amplifier. Mom was whispering sweet nothings into her boyfriend's microphone, unaware that everyone could hear her (quite loudly). They talked about sex (he had an operation which would make intercourse highly improbable) but she didn't mind. She sang to him. When he told her he couldn't dance, she said she'd dance for him (and apparently did).

When your business is taking care of profoundly demented people, it's joyful when a little miracle like this unfolds. It makes everyone happy. So Mom has brought a new vibe to her residence and everyone seems to love her.

On Thursday, I called to see how Mom was doing. Are she and Alan[12] still an item? He was in the hospital. Oh crap, no.

---

[12] Not his real name.

I experienced some angst over that information, and prayed for Alan's swift recovery. Friday, I called and spoke to Mom briefly. She sounded pretty good. More lucid than usual. She said she wanted to go home soon and had resumed packing.[13] Hmm.

Then the director of the home called me. She told me Alan was back and he's fine. Mom, however, had an altercation with a new female resident who also found Alan irresistible. They wrestled a bit and Mom got bruised wrists, but she's fine. I was also assured that, at the time of day I called, all the residents say they want to "go home." It's part of "sundowning."[14]

What's really cool is Alan wants to be with Mom. He was supposed to be transferred to a facility for higher-functioning people, but he's decided to stay specifically to be with Mom. He's asked for privacy with her. He's not at all interested in anyone else. And Mom now calls him by *his name* (not "Herby"). She knows who he is and it appears their romance is *real* (today). True love in a group home. Who'd've thunk it?

---

[13] "Packing" is an activity which became habitual and troublesome with my mother. Mom would "pack" her suitcase, hiding and destroying a lot of her personal effects (like when she ripped the temples off her reading glasses). She would forget and accuse people of "stealing" these "packed" items from her. She often used Poise pads and diapers as packing material.

[14] "Sundowning" is a term that refers to the propensity of the demented to undergo behavioral changes when the sun gets lower in the sky. Part of this is attributed to the way sunlight impacts mood in many individuals. My own theory is that medications taken earlier in the day are also wearing off as evening approaches.

CHAPTER 26:
"UNFORGETTABLE"

July 19, 2011

Saturday was a great day. We went into the city with our nieces and took the Water Taxi around New York Harbor in glorious weather. The youngest of the three just turned 21 and she's working at Columbia University. We took them out for dinner after the cruise at a favorite eatery near the Seaport and had a really nice time.

On Sunday, Bob and I had planned to sail, but we got a really late start. One of our nieces stayed over, I got a call from a dear old friend, and we weren't ready to go until after 2:30. I had been planning to visit Mom and maybe introduce myself to her new fella. I even put on a dress. After that the plan was to stop home before our sail so we could change our clothes and gather provisions for our outing.

When we got to Mom's latest place, one male resident was sitting outside in the summer heat with a family member. He gave us a friendly greeting. As we entered, Mom was asking one of the caretakers if Tracey had arrived yet. "I'm here now, Mom."

She turned to me and beamed. She was nicely made up and looked good. As we completed our hug, I was approached by one of the caregivers. Could she talk to me, privately? Uh oh.

We ducked into the tiny office and she handed me one of Mom's eyeglass cases. In an inside pocket was a fold of bills. Over three hundred dollars. Holy crap. She's unbelievable!

"She knows exactly how much is there, so please tell her I gave it to you."

I told her I absolutely would. She certainly didn't need all that. Hey, what was going on with Mom and Alan?

"She prefers Frank[15] now."

Huh? Really?

"Your mom's a 'play-ah,'" she grinned broadly.

I must confess I was mighty disappointed, but not really surprised. How can anyone you just met be "unforgettable" when you have short-term memory loss? I didn't even want to know who the other guy was. At this point, Mom's more fickle than a high school cheerleader, so whatever works for her is fine by me.

I showed Mom the money retrieved from her glass case and told her I'd hold it for her. She said she'd need it if she went to one of those stores she liked. I told her if she needed anything, I'd make sure she'd have it.

A female resident shuffled over to our table. Mom warned me to remove my bag from her reach. This person is clearly much further gone than Mom, although she appears to be considerably younger. Mom alluded to the woman's obvious need for a brassiere, but this was probably the least of her problems. She was downright spooky and, sadly, a harbinger of things to come.

Mom told us the place had an elevator that went up to all six floors. In my reality, the house has a staircase and two floors. She also said the actress Julia Roberts had come by

---

[15] Not his real name.

to visit her and told her that women have the same right to sexual pleasure as men. Nice of Julia to take time out of her busy schedule to advise my mother on her love life.

We wrapped up our visit telling Mom we were going sailing. Once we got to the car, Bob said he couldn't sail. He was exhausted. He feels bad for Mom.

I asked him if he had any reservations about the place she was in, and he didn't. It's just tough to watch where she's headed.

We went home, holding fast to the great memories of the weekend, hoping to minimize the sadness of our latest visit to the land of the lost.

CHAPTER 27:
PRIDE IN THE NAME OF LOVE

July 20, 2011

The calls are starting to come from Mom's friends and relatives. I disconnected Mom's phone at the ALF last Monday and I haven't had the chance to call folks to give them the heads up about where she's gone, and why. For the most part, people understand that I have been too caught up in facilitating these changes to call individuals to inform them. If everyone who cared used email, it would make this easier. Many do not, so when they try to call Mom and get the disconnect message, they call me.

One of Mom's friends from her Florida days, a lady Bob and I love dearly, called yesterday. We talked for a good long time. She had visited us back in February, about a week before Mom fell out of bed. She admitted to being disturbed by the visit, not so much by Mom's mental state, but because of how she looked. Mom always took pride in her appearance, applying her makeup just so, styling her hair, and putting together nice outfits. The day of their visit, Mom clearly wasn't hitting her usual notes, and it was painful for her friend to witness. The realization that her dear friend was morphing into a different person was hard for her and she couldn't get it out of her mind.

I gave her the synopsis of the last few months and Mom's adventures through rehab, the psych hospital, ERs, and ALFs. She was very sympathetic, and was kind enough to ask how I was doing. Truth be told, I'm a lot better now than I was before Mom was transferred to Potomac. There haven't been any frantic calls to action. I feel like she's in the right setting and being cared for appropriately. And I'm taking way better care of myself.

One of the nicest things she said to me was, "I'm so proud of you." These are words I've had to pry from the jaws of my own family members over the years. Compliments never flowed in our house.

This reminded me of an incident, back when Dad was still alive but very ill and living with me, when I called Mom out on this duality; I knew she often bragged about me to friends and family, but she could never say it directly to me. And her pride in me did *not* translate to her actions. She was often rude to me and very demanding. I had finally reached my limit.

I told her that she had to understand that Herb was my father and this was hard for me, too. While losing a spouse is admittedly much harder than losing a parent, it still hurts, and I was doing the best I could. And then I told her that I knew she was proud of me only because others had told me that she had expressed it to them. But she *never said it to me*.

"And the way you treat me doesn't exactly communicate pride either, Mom. Can you try to be a *little* nicer to me?"

She looked down at the floor and nodded. She got it. She would try.

Mom's friend closed our conversation saying, "I know, one day before she passes to a better life, your mother will tell you she's proud of you."

Well, there's telling and there's showing. In my mother's current confusion and paranoia, one thing has remained consistent: she trusts me. If I tell her something, she never argues, but accepts what I say. So if she never does say the actual words before she gets to the other side, I will always take pride in knowing that I always did my best for her and she knew it, no matter what. I can live with that. I am proud of myself.

CHAPTER 28:
UNEXPECTED
DIVIDENDS

July 29, 2011

As Bob and I were watching a movie at home the other night, my cell buzzed with a text message from my brother. Would I like him to pack up Mom's remaining clothes at the old ALF on Sunday? I replied, "That would be awesome."

As detailed in Chapter 17, when I sold Mom's apartment in Florida back in April, I got stuck doing the whole wretched thing mostly on my own. My brother, who had promised to come, had backed out at the last minute for business reasons. I was physically exhausted and emotionally drained by the experience. My anger with my brother had less to do with his absence and more to do with the way he neglected to tell me until it was too late for me to do anything but soldier through alone. I couldn't even talk to him, because I *knew* he would turn the situation around on me and make me the villain. It's how he operates. He acts as if the self-inflicted pain of feeling guilty should be punishment enough. I had written him a letter (the printed kind in an envelope with a stamp) asking that he deal with the next move (which I presumed, at the time, would be from the ALF to the funeral home). He got angry, turned it around on me, and said a lot of nasty things that made me realize how deep his resentment runs and how irrational he is.

I pulled away. I had no intention of having any further interactions with him. However, I suffer from a pathological need to take the high road. Whenever Mom's situation changed, I would let him know. He may not be much of a brother to me, but he's still my mother's son. He has a right to know where she is and why, so I keep him apprised.

He seems to think all is forgiven as I am cordial when we speak, but it's not. I have very low expectations and have no feelings of obligation to maintain the illusion of closeness. I respond when contacted. I disseminate as necessary.

So the offer of help is appreciated. But there's a little trepidation. Is he doing this to be kind, or is this a treasure hunt?

"If he's looking for money, he's SOL,"[16] chuckled Mom as I told her of Sonny-boy's offer during our visit on Saturday. Bob and I shared meaningful eye contact. We all had the same thought. Mom adores her son, but she knows him all too well.

I sent texts to my brother asking him to put certain items aside for Mom as he packed the apartment. These served as reminders of his promise, as well as specific calls to action on Mom's behalf. At Mom's new home, no coffee is served, only tea. She wanted instant coffee and I knew she had some at her apartment. I also asked that he store most of her clothes in his home in case she wanted anything specific in the future. I'd let him decide which of the multiples to retain or discard.

On Sunday afternoon, Bob and I decided to go to the movies. It was a hot and rainy day, and there was one film I actually did want to see. As we approached the theater,

---

[16] "Shit Out of Luck"

my brother's texts started. He was at the apartment with my sister-in-law. He was concerned about Mom's missing engagement ring.

We conferred about what to store, what to chuck and what to leave for my niece, who was coming for the bedroom set and household items on the following Thursday. I told him we were going to the movies. He asked that I go silent rather than turn off the phone for a little while just in case he needed my input.

While the previews were still rolling, he called. "We found the ring!" Mom had stowed it in a cloth jewelry pouch with some earrings. Wow. Who figured on that? He said he'd put it in a safe for her. Fine by me. If she wanted it, he'd be able to give it to her.

So, the last of the moving will be done later this week by my niece, her boyfriend, and Bob. Whatever's left will be charitable donations and crumbs. This time, all I have to do is the final walk through. For once, maybe I'll come out on the plus side of the metaphysical balance sheet. This morning I found that I'm still not in menopause after a three-month vacation from "The Curse." We'll see what other treats the rest of this week has in store.

CHAPTER 29:
SO MOVING

August 3, 2011

After my brother's visit to pack up the apartment, I got a text from him indicating he'd forgotten Mom's walker. I told him I'd get it. I also wanted to see where we were.

I got to the apartment and there were three large bags marked "Clothes For Donation." Okay, they'd done that much, but they couldn't actually remove and donate the items. Oh well, Bob can toss these in donation bins once he's done helping the kids with the furniture. Don't agitate, delegate.

The drawers and closets had been emptied of clothes and shoes. Hangers, furniture, sundries, and bric-a-brac remained. Not bad. My niece would take a lot of it.

On Wednesday evening, the kids arrived: our niece, her boyfriend, and his identical twin brother. My niece confided that the brother didn't have too many opportunities for fun. He'd just finished his Master's degree and didn't have much money. She asked his help with the move and offered him the "royal treatment" at our place as a perk.

I don't know if the boys find the hot tub quite as appealing as the girls do, but the opportunity to drink beer, soak, and hang out with a beautiful girl in a bikini can't be too hard to take. It was a really nice evening with a clear sky and a beautiful starscape.

My plans for the next day included a business meeting in New Brunswick and a morning meeting of a more personal nature, so I got up early, made two pots of coffee, and tended to my morning tasks. I figured it would be best if I headed to the apartment first while Bob and the kids picked up the moving truck.

I bagged up the linens and towels, disassembled the mirror from the dresser, grabbed a few odds and ends, and called Bob. They were fifteen minutes away. I had to go to my first appointment.

Once at the business meeting, I heard from my niece. Everything went smoothly and they were on their way to her old apartment to empty that place. She was thrilled with the furniture and promised to send pictures when everything was set up.

I took one last look the following Sunday, the last day of the month. I took a few items I had left for my niece. I left some dishes and cups for the next tenant. My work there was done.

Now, to deal with the bills for all of Mom's medications and treatments. Every place she went, a month's worth of drugs was ordered, whether she stayed a week or a day. The "co-pays" are murder. Without insurance, it would be Armageddon.

And I still haven't gotten a cent back from Mom's long-term care since April. She's moved around so much, they haven't been able to nail down the documentation they need to approve the claim. I keep calling and following up.

Meanwhile, Mom's unhappy at the new place and wants to "go home." I seek the advice of the pros, and I am told that the best thing to do is redirect her. Change the subject. Bring her food she likes. Lipstick. Perfume. Photos. Remember, you're dealing with someone who is child-like, not the person they used to be. Don't succumb to guilt. Guilt? Really? After everything I've done, is it possible to feel guilty? Apparently, it's a recessive Semitic trait.

I visited Mom and brought her toothbrushes, some good, fresh food, and a jar of decaf. She's been thinking; she liked the other place better. She wants to go back.

"You can't go back, Mom. They gave your apartment to someone else. They couldn't care for you. You kept trying to run away."

"No I didn't. I was just trying to look around outside."

"Look, you've only been here three weeks. Give it a chance."

"I've been here for months!"

"No, you haven't. You moved in Monday, July 11. Today is Tuesday, August 2. Yesterday was three weeks."

"No way. You made that up."

"We went sailing Saturday. Want to see?"

I showed her some video I shot on my iPhone.

"Oh, that looks beautiful."

I showed her a few more pictures and she was satisfied. She suggested I had other places to go. There's the Jewish mother I know!

I told her if she needed anything, she could have one of the ladies call me for her. I assured her it was okay to call me, and I would see that whatever she needed was provided. I promised to bring her a notebook and pens so she could write stuff down. And she'll lose them and blame someone else. The dance continues. I have nothing to feel guilty about.

The big problem I have is, as psychotic as Mom may be, she's still more lucid than any of the other residents. And she's still enough like her old self to tug at my heartstrings and make me feel like I put her in this place prematurely. But what choice do I have? Move her to another place, roll up the score with another twenty thousand dollars down the drain and find she hates the next place too? Or start getting the crazed phone calls again, that she's acting out and needs restraints or more hands-on care? If I continue to be reactive to her demands, I'll have plowed through all the money before the five-year look-back period elapses. Then what?

My husband assured me today that I've done the right thing and can't keep moving her. My brother told me earlier in the week he was on the same page. I still want professional opinions. Seeing her surrounded by full-time, full-blown psychotics is hard for me to watch. It's really got to suck for Mom. But will I be moved to move her yet again?

CHAPTER 30:
NOT GUILTY

August 8, 2011

As we left Mom on Sunday, I felt terrible. We had taken her out for a nice lunch, and she practically begged me to move her back to the last residence. "Of course they all love me here. I'm the only normal one in the place."

It was a hot, muggy day and I was grateful for the air-conditioning in the restaurant, even in my sleeveless summer dress. Mom was freezing in her long-sleeved blouse and denim jacket. She had done up her hair. She looked nice. I was buying into the illusion of her "normalcy." I had a tough time eating my meal, good as it was.

Bob chatted amiably with Mom, telling her about our travels, fun with the nieces, sailing on our boat, happenings with his friends, coworkers, and bandmates. Mom tried to respond appropriately and did pretty well.

I had Mom's leftovers and mine packed up. The portions were huge, and the food was delicious and fresh, so I felt certain that she'd get several good meals out of them.

We drove around and showed Mom the area she was living in. She was impressed with the beauty of the surroundings. But she wasn't looking forward to going back to the residence.

Upon our return, I handed the boxes of food to one of the caregivers and she assured me they'd warm them for Mom whenever she wanted. It was 4:30 and they were already eating dinner. I couldn't quite make out what they were eating, but Mom insisted they were getting a lot of rice and beans to control costs. (She had similar complaints at the other places she'd stayed, too, so a grain of salt must be taken.) She also told me she was not taking her morning meds so she could stay awake during the day, although there wasn't much reason for her to stay up. No activities interested her. All they do is play Bingo. Nothing on TV that she liked. No movies. (I had meant to bring DVDs for her to watch! Damn! I remembered the Poise pads, but forgot the entertainment!)

Mom suggested Bob and I leave. She didn't want to take up any more of our time. But she made another case for moving: "I know I heard her say, 'Rosalind, I forgive you.' Maybe she'll reconsider?"

This was Mom's belief that one of her delusional creations was responsible for her having to leave the last place. There was no point in trying to correct this. No one threw her out or blamed her for anything. They simply could not provide the kind of care Mom needed at the last place. Here, they can. But she didn't know what she had lost until it was gone. Sorry, Ma.

Looking around the place, it was obvious that Mom was indeed the most able and lucid resident. Several new folks had arrived in the last couple of weeks, and none seemed nearly as alert or verbal as my mother. One in particular really ticks Mom off. She has no boundaries, so I really get why Mom hates her. Mom curses at her and has said repeatedly that she popped her in the jaw. I still don't know for sure whether that really happened.

On the way home, Bob knew I was troubled. "Maybe she can be moved to a facility for higher functioning people?" I thought out loud.

"You can't keep moving her."

"I know."

"You did the right thing."

"I know. But it still hurts me to see her in that situation. I want professionals to tell me she's in the right place."

When we got home, I emailed "Julia Roberts" and told her what Mom had said and asked about options. She replied that she'd be in Montville today (Monday) and would call me from there.

My kitty, Cody, spent much of the night with me. He cuddled and tickled my face with his paw as I slept. Funny how pets pick up on our emotions.

In the morning, I reached out and got some supportive feedback. The term "guilt" comes up more often than I'd like, though. *I am not guilty.* I have no reason to feel guilty. I have repeatedly gone above and beyond on her behalf. What I do feel is compassion.

It's terrible that Mom has to be in a place where everyone else is so much less able than she is. It's like being a sixth grader plunked down in a kindergarten class. Mom's social worker liked this analogy. He called me today, at "Julia's" request.

This social worker is a "peer" of Mom's, someone older but lucid, qualified, and employed as a therapist/sounding board/support system for residents like my mother. He visits weekly and had seen Mom last week. He was sympathetic and told me that Mom was one of 100 percent of residents who wanted out of their facilities. They all want to "go home." That's just a given.

But what about someone like Mom who's psychotic, but still so relatively self-sufficient and articulate? Isn't it right for her to feel misplaced? She isn't like the rest. She has so little to occupy her. Isn't it too soon for her to be in this particular setting?

He agreed that Mom was indeed more lucid, but she did clearly need to be watched, right? Haven't her doctors and caregivers determined this need?

I explained Mom's recent adventures in psychiatry and violence. There have been many doctors attending to her and trying to strike a balance of medication and appropriate setting. It has not been easy. I chose Potomac because it was pretty much the one place that would have her. Other places are too big, potentially inciting her paranoia and violent behavior. The best thing that can be said about her current location is I haven't gotten a single panicked call for intervention since she moved in four weeks ago. That's a new record since this phase began.

My Monday morning included a visit to my chiropractor. Since stress affects the spine (and because I can't exactly hide my inner torment), I told the doctor what was going on. He, too, was sympathetic. Don't we all deal with this to some degree? He told me his father was a very strong-willed man. When he started developing dementia, he went to bed one night and didn't wake up. He willed himself to die. Boy, that's willpower! He told me to remember that I was doing my best and that's all anyone can do.

Once at home from my errands, I sat down at my computer to write out my angst, and a message from my very dear friend was bouncing in my browser. This friend from high school, more a brother to me than anyone else in my life, has always been tuned in to my "cosmic cries for help." Today was no different. We chatted for an hour and a half.

As I was sitting down for a late lunch, Bob called. He knew I was hurting. He just wanted to see how I was.

Another call came from a woman who is setting up Mom's evaluation at Potomac for her long-term care claim. Another reason I can't move her. She has to stay put long enough for her claim to finally be settled.

And "Julia" called. She spent some quality time with Mom. She spoke with her caregivers and her more lucid housemates. Mom is actually doing fine. She has her own routine. She's not acting out, is taking her meds, and isn't showing signs of anything negative. She is acclimating. And some new residents who are more on Mom's level are coming in shortly. That's welcome news.

What it all comes down to is, someone has to be the grown-up. Grown-up decisions are not easy. I took on this job, and I'm doing it to the best of my ability. There are no easy answers, no perfect situations. Compromises must be struck. Accommodations must be made. And I have to hold on to one irrefutable reality: my mother has dementia and psychosis; she needs to be watched and cared for; she is in a place that provides care and security. Now I need to find the peace that comes from accepting that, and the strength to continue facing my mother, no matter what she ultimately becomes.

Can I go home now?

CHAPTER 31:
VESTIGIAL
IMPULSES

August 14, 2011

As I set about the mindless task of changing my bed linens, I had a sudden urge to call Mom. Not Mom at Potomac, but independent Mom in Florida. Back in the days immediately following my father's demise, I would call my mother at least once a week to check on her. She would often conclude our calls by saying how much she enjoyed our "visits." It gave her particular pleasure when I called her; she felt no sense of "intruding" on me, and was pleased that I elected to call her. She always preferred it that way. Mom was never much for reaching out, but enjoyed being reached.

A similar phenomenon occurred with my father too. I began mourning his loss acutely the year before he actually passed away. I spent a great deal of time navigating his deterioration. I'd had a unique relationship with him. He liked and respected me as an adult. I valued his point of view. I loved sharing events of my life with him. His interest in computers, which he pursued in his seventies, allowed us to form a new and different bond. He was one of my most entertaining and motivated students. His sense of humor and desire to help us through difficult times can't be overstated. When he started losing his mind, it was devastating for all of us. Even while he was in the throes of vascular dementia, the impulse to call the old Herby would hit me, and I would realize the futility of my wish. Seven years after his physical death, I still miss him. I continue to converse with him in my mind, trying to conjure what his response would be to a particular situation.

It really isn't a linear path. That's a large part of what makes this so difficult. Humans are so complex. The condition of our brains plays such a profound role in who we are from day to day, moment to moment. I have placed my mother in a facility equipped to deal with her condition as it changes. Their goal is to help her stay as high-functioning, and on as few drugs, as possible. It seems they are managing her well, but in her state of mind, my mother doesn't appreciate it. And there's the rub. The better they care for her, the better she feels, and the less acceptable she finds it to be where she is.

In time, Mom's condition will worsen. It's inevitable. Eventually, she probably won't care where she is as her psychosis and dementia take over. I don't look forward to the time when she no longer knows me, but I accept it as a likely part of the process. I want to see her while she's still able to relate to me, but I dread her complaints and requests to be moved someplace else. The longer she stays put, the better she will acclimate and hopefully, become more accepting. She's safe. She's functioning. She is making friends. And I'm able to care for myself, my husband, my business, my pets, and other obligations with a clearer head. In time, the urge to connect with independent, lucid Mom will probably fade too. I'm starting to miss her already.

CHAPTER 32:
BEE HERE NOT

August 18, 2011

Never count on life getting easier. Ever.

I live in a beautiful area. It's almost rural. We're surrounded by trees, lakes, mountains, reservoirs, and lots of critters. This past spring, we had a carpenter ant invasion. It's happened before, and at the first sign of them, I called in the pros. I don't want anything eating my house. When you live in a town like Ringwood, you are constantly reminded that Nature wants your house back. From black bears to raccoons, to ants and other pests, they're always around and vigilance is mandatory.

When I hired my current exterminator service, I had invited two companies to quote on the ant problem. The first quote was in line with others I'd received in the past. The second guy came and said they'd not only treat the ant problem, but would come back and deal with any other pests that plagued us, like bees.

Bees! Yes! Every spring, bees start getting into my house. I have floor to ceiling windows in my living room, and they seemed to come in through the window frames. I'd go through long periods where there were no bees in evidence, and then, suddenly, I'd start seeing many. Not swarms, but maybe six a day. I'd spray them with peppermint oil and they'd fall. I hate that stuff, though. While it's supposedly safe for pets and the environment, it smells like peppermint (which isn't a favorite of mine) and the oil runs all over the place. It's really tough to clean, particularly off glass. But better annoyed than stung, and I don't want my kitties to get sick.

Last week, the summer bee surge began and I called for reinforcements. I phoned on Thursday. They gave me an appointment for Monday afternoon between 1 and 5. Oh well, we'll do our best until then.

Friday, I coped. Since they congregate in the kitchen and living room, I can hide out in my office. Saturday, Bob and I had a concert in Manhattan, so we left early and dined out. Sunday, the bees went from surge to siege. They were all over the kitchen. Bob went outside and found the probable entry point: an old exhaust vent that had been closed but pried open enough to admit bees. Bob sprayed the last of the peppermint oil in the hole and closed it up with duct tape and Gorilla Glue.

The bees continued to come inside. They would emerge from the under-cabinet lights and fly up to the kitchen skylight. They'd fly through the beam space from the kitchen toward the bright light of the living room windows. Bee carcasses dropped everywhere.

I went to the supermarket and bought more bee spray. This time I grabbed the black can rather than the green. I meant business. I wanted these varmints dead (and less peppermint grease dripping).

The new spray was helpful, but Bob continued to swat at the intruders, finishing the job the sprays started. He worked up quite a sweat. Meanwhile, I got the bucket and mop and cleaned up the dripping insecticide. There were still bees coming in, but they were clearly staggering from the poison, proving easy to smack between mop strokes.

Bob and I cleaned up and went out for lunch. Upon our return, dead bees littered the floor, countertops and sink. "It's Beemageddon!" I called to Bob as I began sweeping up the carnage.

As the evening approached, the buzzing activity stopped and we were able to watch TV in peace. I could get drinks and snacks from the kitchen without my skin crawling. Bob thought he'd solved the problem. I was quietly glad the pros were coming.

Monday morning, more dead bees graced the floor of the kitchen and buzzed about as I tried to make coffee. Armed with the black can, rolled up newspaper, and dust pan with brush, I killed a bunch more and got the coffee going. I went downstairs to feed the cats and came back up to find many more bees in the living room and kitchen.

I called the service and begged the operator to get a guy over as quickly as the schedule would allow. I haven't been able to wash my dishes or make a salad all weekend. I'm too creeped out and afraid I will eventually get stung. Boy, am I glad Mom's not here for this.

At 2 p.m., I had a teleconference scheduled for the planning of a real-life industry conference in 2012. Of course, the exterminator arrived about fifteen minutes in. I muted the call while the others carried on, blissfully unaware of my situation. When I showed the tech the affected areas of my home, the color drained out of his face. I knew I was in trouble.

I showed him where Bob had intervened at the back of the house. Once he got started, he saw something had been put in there to plug the hole. I called Bob at work. Yeah, he used Gorilla Glue. Not good. Bob had sealed in a great big honkin' nest of yellow jackets. Now their only way out was into the kitchen. Yikes! Bob spoke with the exterminator who went back outside to attack the problem. I returned to the safety of my office and resumed active participation in the conference call.

The poor guy got stung, but he also got to the nest. He was able to create an opening and shoot in his magical white powder. We could see the bees flying around, looking like they'd been to a cocaine party. They were dropping, but they were still coming out from their hideout. The kitchen sink, countertops, kitchen floor, living room floor, and windowsills were strewn with bee carcasses. He assured me they'd all be dead by tomorrow. If any survived, call the office. Someone would return to finish the job if necessary. Meanwhile, use the black can (and I could see the pro had resorted to it himself).

I called Bob and asked him to bring home another black can. I told him I'd clean up best I could, but there were still enough live bees around to prevent me from making a salad and a proper dinner. And the house stank of insecticide. I would open the doors and windows to exhaust the fumes and lock the kitties downstairs in safety until the poison dissipated. Maybe we should dine out tonight? I didn't want to, but the buzzing of the dying-but-still-living bees persuaded me to say *yes*.

Then the sky opened up. I had seen a weather report that morning about flash floods in lower lying areas. Thank God I live in the mountains. The rain rolls off our house, down the storm drains, and into the reservoirs. Sorry about the bee killer stuff in the water supply, folks. Couldn't "bee" avoided!

The rain was coming down so hard I had to close everything to just a crack. So much for aerating the fumes.

At least the exterminator got to us before the deluge. It really would have sucked to have to deal with the bees during the torrential downpour.

Tuesday morning I awoke and tentatively looked around. More bee carcasses littered the living room. A couple of writhers were still in their death throes; a couple of dead ones lay on the kitchen floor. I listened for buzzing. I started to make coffee. I went down to feed the kitties and decided it was safe to let them come back upstairs.

Returning to the kitchen to make my breakfast, I started making some calls. Mom still has not been evaluated at her new group home. The long-term care insurance folks need to assess the appropriateness of the new facility for the insured's condition. I was given another number: the people they hire to hire the people who do the assessments. I called the person in charge of Mom's case and left a voice mail. A lovely associate of hers called me back.

As I explained my mother's situation to this new contact, I saw Cody, my kitten, in rapt attention to something in the living room. You guessed it. More live bees. Seven of them.

I managed not to freak out, but once I concluded that call, I rang the exterminators. A nice fellow answered and said these were probably stragglers who had not returned to the nest. I told him they were a lot more lively than the ones I'd found earlier this morning and that the tech who'd been out yesterday told me they should all be dead by now. He said no problem, and he could have someone come back this morning. Awesome!

Meanwhile, out came the rolled up newspaper, black can, and cleaning implements. I smacked the ones I could reach, sprayed the ones I couldn't. I left the corpses out for the tech to see.

I went to work, listening for the doorbell. By noon, no one had come. "Oh, you're not on the schedule. And it takes 24 to 48 hours for the insecticide to work. But I'll put you on the schedule for tomorrow morning." Swell. At least now I can get my day going. I swept up the dead bees, cleaned up the dripping spray, looked for more live ones and, finding none (except for an apparently-dead bee butt hanging out from an under-cabinet light fixture in the kitchen), I dumped the refuse and tentatively planned the rest of my day.

Desperately needing a non-bee-related workout, I got my athletic gear on and got going downstairs. As I got to the cooldown, I could see a man at my door. It was another extermination tech.

"I thought you were coming tomorrow morning."

"Oh? Well, what's going on?"

I escorted him up the stairs and gave him "the buzz." No bees were apparent. It was looking good. I showed him the outside and returned the tools his colleague had left behind to him. He said he'd call me in the morning to check and see if the call was still necessary.

"If you hear screaming, please come back."

He smiled and said he would.

This morning, no bees, dead or alive. The nurse scheduled to assess Mom just called; she's delayed at a doctor's appointment, but she'll be there. The long-term care (LTC) insurance carrier has finally issued the first of many pending reimbursement checks for Mom's care. The sun is shining. And I am feeling a whole lot better. Time to buzz off!

CHAPTER 33:
POOR KID

August 24, 2011

"So you've got it on both sides? Oh my God, you poor kid!" The haircutter was digesting the conversation we'd been having about my lifelong bouts of caregiving as she feathered my bangs. I had started with Mom, gone back to Dad and explained how I'd even been my husband's caregiver, seeing him through cancer after we'd been dating for about a year. But the fact that I had two parents who each had dementia was a noteworthy predicament.

"My father's dementia was apparently vascular – he had lots of small strokes going off in his brain. His was related to coronary artery disease, which came from his lifestyle. My mother's is most likely Alzheimer's. It runs in her family. But it won't happen to me."

"You've thought about it?"

"Of course. I know exactly what I'll do. I won't hang around. When I stop being the person I value being, I will end it."

And I mean it. At fifty-three, I am an active person who works to stay fit. I am doing everything in my power to prevent the onset of dementia. I'm hopeful I can hold it off with a healthy lifestyle. But I'm not arrogant enough to think there's any way to ensure that I will escape my parents' fate. The current research is improving the outlook, but the genetic dice may already be cast.

I don't have children. I do have three nieces who might be inclined to help me should I start to slip.[17] However, I have no intention of ever putting them in that position. Knowing that the odds are somewhat against me, I am prepared to face the truth head on.

I will be vigilant. I will take care of myself and enjoy my life to the fullest. I will be on guard against the early warning signs. And if I ever get a second opinion indicating the imminent demise of my brain, I will go before it's too late.

I've always had great instincts about when to leave a party. Drifting off blissfully to oblivion in my sleep, unassisted, is a gift I dare not even consider receiving. I don't know anyone who's enjoyed that blessing. Not even a pet.

I'd like to leave this soiree at 102, after taking a magnificent dump in my own bathroom, having consumed a delicious breakfast made with my own two hands, from a recipe I know by heart. Checking on me after doing the breakfast dishes, my adorable and faithful thirty-six-year-old boyfriend finds me stiff, cold, and smiling on the bathroom floor. Poor kid.

---

[17] One of my dear nieces has consented to be my appointed advocate. My husband is my healthcare proxy, but if anything happens to him, my niece has agreed to fill that role for me (and for my husband should I not be there for him). Everyone should designate advocates. *Everyone.*

CHAPTER 34:
PLAYING WITH MATCHES

September 2, 2011

"How did you find me?" Mom was surprised and pleased that I'd arrived. It was the Friday before Hurricane Irene, and I wanted to see her before we got hit. No telling when I'd be able to get back there for another visit and I wanted to check on the storm plans at the facility.

"I always know where you are, Ma. Julia Roberts keeps me informed. Did you go somewhere?"

"Yeah, we were down at my old place the last couple of days."

"Barnegat?"

"No, Florida."

Hmm. She went on to explain how she and several of the residents had been taken to a hotel in her old town in Florida and she was very impressed with the arrangements. Everything was smooth. And now she was here. Wherever "here" is.

She had a lovely hairdo. I arranged for her hair to be cut and styled at the next visit from the stylist, and Mom was freshly coiffed. She was feeling pretty well except for her big toes.[18] That meant her gout was flaring up and of course, she told no one but me. I went to speak with the nurse on duty and asked her to please make sure Mom got her anti-inflammatory medication. I reviewed Mom's drug list with the nurse and located the right prescription. I also filled her in on the dosing schedule; "as needed" doesn't exactly cut it.

I returned to sit with Mom and another resident's child came in. Ah, the daughter of Mom's arch-nemesis, Janie.[19] This is the woman with whom Mom came to blows her first week in Montville. She's a lot further gone than Mom, and has no boundaries. She takes things that don't belong to her and Mom says she steals from her room. Recently, a new fellow came to live at the home and he and Janie became a couple. They sit together and hold hands. Janie also likes to carry a baby doll around.

There's another female resident who is barely verbal. She attached herself to another new male resident and Mom gave me some of the gory details of their liaisons. Eww, Mom, please, too much information. She grinned and welcomed me to her world. Sorry, Mom. But I've got to say that fellow had a great big grin on his face. Lord knows how he's processing the receipt of such pleasure, but he doesn't seem to be suffering.

I put on a movie for the folks: *Some Like It Hot*. Mom was surprised that it was black and white. I kissed her goodbye and left her marveling at how gorgeous Tony Curtis had been.

---

[18] What I did not know then was Mom's gout in her big toe was also a symptom of Polycythemia Vera.

[19] Not her real name.

Out in the parking lot, Janie's daughter was leaving too. I introduced myself and we traded backstories on our mothers and concerns about the coming storm. Janie had also been thrown out of her last home for violent behavior and acting out. We laughed as I indicated that I was pretty sure that our mothers had engaged in some "rock 'em sock 'em" action with each other.

Janie's daughter also told me something interesting about the newfound relationship. Her mother thinks the new beau is her dead husband, and that's pretty much what you'd expect. However, the gentleman in question thinks her mother is his brother. He refers to her as "he" and is very protective of "him." It's fascinating how delusional folks find each other and satisfy their basic need for human contact with someone who fleshes out the phantoms in their heads, lending reality to their fantasies.

Just as Mom thought Alan[20] was Herby at first, she believed a variety of different people she encountered in her adventures had some kind of relationship with her, regardless of their actual gender or disposition. I'm starting to think that old Stephen Stills song *Love the One You're With* has some implications beyond the free-love anthem it was surely meant to be.

If you can't be with the one you love, honey
Love the one you're with

Here's hoping that wherever you are, you're safe, dry, and feeling gratitude for the life you have. And if you're not, may you find what you need in whatever or whoever comes your way next.

---

[20] Not his real name.

CHAPTER 35:
THE "F" WORD

September 15, 2011

There's a topic I have waltzed around in my posts, but I've decided it's time to address it head on. Participating in a project designed to aid caregivers, I recently watched a video focused on people who oversee their loved-ones' care, and something really hit home: when you're in the thick of prioritizing another person's well-being over your own, you tend to become thick yourself. You don't eat consciously or make time for exercise. So the "F" word I'm talking about here is a three-letter one: *fat*.

I have fought being overweight my whole life. Starting with my mother being summoned by the school nurse, I was deemed unhealthily overweight at ten. I began my first official diet, counting calories, when I was in the fifth grade. My weight decreased, and I earned kudos from neighbors and friends, but I always fluctuated. I swung up and down, unable to maintain control in a household of overeaters. Entenmann's cakes were always in the kitchen "just in case" we had company. My mother always gave me mixed messages: "Don't you *dare* eat that!" followed by "What's the matter? Why aren't you eating?"

When I got to college, I lived at home, but spent much of my time away, exerting more control over my food choices and activities. I moved out when I graduated, at twenty.

Through adulthood, I continued the struggle to find sustainable ways to be healthy.

I got married at thirty-three in a size 16 wedding dress. (I am 5'2", so it should have been a 4 or a 6.) When I saw the videos of our honeymoon hike up Dunn's River Falls playing on an endless loop in our hotel lobby in Jamaica, I was mortified. I signed up for Nutrisystem when I got home. I learned better habits and portion control. I lost thirty-five pounds in 1992, achieving the healthy size 4 body I sought.

Maintenance worked for me as long as I charted my food and exercise. After about three years, I got cocky and thought I was done having to watch myself. Big mistake.

I eventually gained all the weight back. Around 2000, I got sick of myself and decided to re-implement my Nutrisystem knowledge, tracking my food and exercise. During the high-stress interval following the 9-11-2001 attacks (I had seen the Towers ablaze driving from my home in New Jersey toward the Lincoln Tunnel, which closed before I could enter it), I resisted the urge to overeat. I told myself, if I screw up, the terrorists win. So I redoubled my efforts and used exercise to battle the stress rather than reach for comfort food. I got back down to my fighting weight again.

In 2003, my dad got sick and I became intimately involved in his care. Moving my folks up to New Jersey from Florida, I had them living with me for a while as I shuttled Dad from doctor to doctor. The more I learned about the gravity of his situation, the more the stress got to me. I saw a therapist and journaled through my misery. I missed workouts. I made poor food decisions.

And here's something interesting about dementia: people who have it develop a wicked sweet tooth. My dad *never* liked sweets before he got sick. He always loved spicy, fatty foods and eating way too much of them, very quickly. His attraction to ice cream and pastries was new. But we all agreed that if that's what made Dad happy, quality of life beat quantity of days, and we indulged him. Being around that, it was often hard to resist imbibing myself (and I have *always* had a sweet tooth).

I hung on, though. I put some weight back on, but not all of it. Until grad school that is.

In 2005, I was accepted to a Master's program at NYU. I went back to school full time at age forty-seven. I gradually fell back into bad old habits. I was in front of computers all the time, sedentary, nurturing my mind, but not my body. I would literally forget to eat and later binge. I paid the price in weight gain and debilitating lower back pain, featuring a summer of chiropractic treatments, doctor visits, and painkillers. By the time I earned my MS in 2007, I had regained all my weight along with my 3.75 GPA.

Again, I fought to get the weight off. I lost about half of what I needed to lose. Then Mom's cognitive status went precipitously southward, and as chronicled here, she came to live with us.

Having one's mother living in their home is challenging enough when the parent is mentally able. Add dementia to the menu, and you've got a recipe for disaster. I tried to cook healthfully for all of us, but it was really hard. I wanted to indulge my husband, who's a steak and potatoes guy. He will only eat poultry if it's deep fried. He likes salads but won't eat most fruits. Mom pretty much ate anything I put in front of her, but as time went on, she needed more help getting it from the plate to her mouth. This influenced the menus too.

I enjoyed all the stuff I cooked and ate way too much of it to fill the aching void in my center. Even with the healthful preparation techniques I'd implement, if you eat too much of anything (which gave me GERD[21], another family curse) and don't exercise enough (I couldn't leave Mom alone long enough to get in regular workouts, right?) you will ingest more calories than you burn, which results in weight gain. It's simple math. Being in perimenopause, with the hormonal surges, mood swings, and slowing metabolism, doesn't help either.

The last straw, for me, was in late April. I was down in Florida, selling my parents' apartment. Staying at a modern hotel, everywhere I looked I saw my reflection, and it wasn't pretty. I didn't just look fat, I looked *old*. I felt ancient. I needed to be retrained. So, one day, as I worked on my laptop in my lovely hotel room with all the stupid mirrors, I made an appointment with a Jenny Craig Center in Wayne, New Jersey, less than a mile from the ALF where Mom was then living.

I started the program in May and set my goal at 30 pounds. I wanted to be in good shape for my twentieth anniversary in late October. Bob and I had decided to go to Hawaii, and I'd be damned if I'd go there and see a video in the lobby of our hotel featuring a huffing-puffing old butterball with my face on it.

Bob has been great about it. He makes his own meals now, so our arguments over what to eat and when have dissipated. And he does like what he sees in me.

Last week, I got on my Wii Fit board, and for the first time since I got the blasted contraption, it did *not* say "That's

---

[21] Gastroesophageal reflux disease, which my father had and my brother has too. Mom has also had ulcers. Since I've changed my lifestyle, all GERD symptoms have abated without drugs.

Overweight!" as it revealed my BMI and weight. It said "*Normal!*" with a burst of fireworks and much rejoicing by my "Mii" (the Wii avatar that represents me). It was the first time I didn't feel like throwing the bloody thing under my car wheels.

I have a ways to go and about six weeks until we leave for Hawaii. I may not get to my ultimate goal weight before we go, but I should be close. Over twenty pounds down and I feel way better. Working out is *so* much easier now that I'm carrying around less weight.

The more important thing, though, is that I finally get this: it's not a temporary thing. It's a process. I can't *ever* stop. I must *always* track my food and exercise. I can eat or drink anything I want to *in moderation*. As long as I do, I will stay where I need to be: healthy, present, mindful, and self-aware. It's my choice.

It is *not* easy. But if you are a caregiver, please don't let your own needs go unheeded for too long, whatever they may be. If you're unhealthy and unhappy, you're of no value to anyone. Figure out how to prioritize your own needs higher. It's a challenge well worth taking. After all, it's your life. Don't "f" it up.

Author's note: I have since stopped consuming Jenny Craig food (or as I have come to call it, "Jenny Crack"). While tasty and convenient, the meals are *loaded* with unhealthy additives, are highly processed, and are rather expensive. I am currently exploring whole foods and organics, favoring a more plant-based diet. The dance continues.

CHAPTER 36:
ALOHA

November 14, 2011

Well, this is a fine how do you do.

For the first time in five years, Bob and I got to take a real vacation. The kind of vacation where you only do things you want to do. No errands for Mom. No crazed phone calls. Just the kind of luxury and fun befitting a twentieth wedding anniversary.

Last year, Bob had forgotten our anniversary. Very unlike him, but under the circumstances, he was very busy at work and I was up to my neck in caregiving. I was sad and vocal about the lack of acknowledgment. Bob apologized and said our twentieth would get its due. We could go wherever I wanted.

Italy! I always wanted to see Florence, where so many of Michelangelo's works were on view. And Venice. And Rome.

Bob agreed. For a while. But then "Arab Spring" began, and refugees from Tunisia and Lebanon began streaming into Italy. Might we consider something else?

Hawaii. I had been to Oahu thirty years ago when I worked for a Japanese travel agency. My alcoholic Japanese boss offered me the trip as a "paid vacation." When I got there, he forced me to work the tour desk every day, helping the incentive trip winners at the resort to enjoy themselves. I got to sit inside watching others having fun. I got one day off to snorkel at Hanauma Bay. It was unforgettable, and I swore I'd one day return as a tourist. This was the time.

I booked a vacation package through AARP/Expedia and got the hotel for eight nights in a King room with breakfast daily, round trip, nonstop air, and a full-size car for one attractive price. The hotel, the Kahala Hotel & Resort, is a five-star gem on the southeastern shore of Oahu, just ten minutes from Waikiki, with its own private beach and lagoon enlivened by five dolphins cavorting with guests (for a fee) and performing tricks just to add to the ambience.

The place was better than you could imagine and we had the time of our lives. We enjoyed the beach and pool just about every day. Our room was lovely, featuring a terrace with a mountain/golf course/waterfall/lagoon/ocean view and a king bed as comfy as our own back home (which is saying something). We scaled Diamond Head, visited the Arizona Memorial, checked out Waikiki, snorkeled at Hanauma Bay, and did a little shopping (it was time to procure my first bikini in many years). I took yoga and Pilates classes on the beach. I kissed and petted a dolphin. We took a sail on a catamaran at sunset and watched fireworks shot from the Hilton Hawaiian Village. We found cool restaurants with delicious food and drinks that were a little more affordable than the offerings at our resort.

One hitch in the proceedings occurred during a visit to the Kahala Mall. We stopped there on our first Saturday. We had toured the northwestern portion of the island in our rented car. I wanted to see if I could find any bathing suits I might like, get a little lunch, and snag some sundries.

The parking lot was busy and we circled a while until we spotted a Japanese family preparing to depart in their parked minivan. The young mother was struggling with the stroller, trying to fold it and put it in the back of the van. The thing was not cooperating. I started making a little fun of the poor gal. (Having worked at a Japanese travel agency, I could still do a really good, cruel impression of Japanese English. "Oh honey, prease hep me wit dis ting! Honeeee!!") Then the husband appears with their baby in his arms. He transfers the child to Mama and she retreats to the vehicle. Papa stomps on the correct release pedal and the stroller yields to his pressure. Into the van goes the folded stroller, followed by Papa-san. Away they go. Bob and I are giggling watching the transaction. It's funny because it's not us.

We parked in the vacated spot. I locked my beach bag holding a couple of digital cameras, my sneakers, hat, socks, the depleted battery case for my iPhone, sunscreen, hotel room key, and a voucher for our Friday night sail in the trunk. Still giggling, we went shopping.

I found my first two-piece bathing suit. It's not easy finding a flattering suit, but after trying on a whole bunch, I settled on one I would not feel bad wearing in public. Then I bought a tossed salad with chicken and ate it at a table outside the Whole Foods store as Bob went inside for a look. By the time he emerged with his purchase, I'd finished my salad. We returned to the car and I asked Bob to open the trunk. The trunk was empty.

Wait a minute. We're on vacation. How could this happen? I called 911 and they sent a squad car right over.

The policeman was nice, but he chastised us for putting the bag in the trunk after we parked, where we could be seen doing it. (I'd never do anything that stupid in Brooklyn.) He went on to explain that the Dodge Charger (our rental) was a notoriously easy car to break into. And ours had been. The driver's side lock had been jimmied. They used the release inside the car to open the trunk and grab my bag. Damn!

I filed a police report and said I would press charges and testify if the thieves were found. Hey, who wouldn't use any excuse to go back to Hawaii?

I also filed a report with mall security. Having reviewed all the items lost, it wasn't that big a deal. It was early in the trip, so I hadn't taken a lot of pictures. And both cameras were older. Everything could be replaced. No IDs were taken. We were lucky.

Since we were at the mall, I figured I might as well replace the more essential items: the sneakers, the iPhone battery case, and the sunscreen. I found a pair of sneakers on sale at Macy's. After getting very discouraged at the teeming Apple Store, I went to the much more accessible Verizon Store and found a battery case for my iPhone (which would now serve as my primary camera). I picked up a fresh tube of water-proof sunscreen and we were ready to head back to the resort.

Once in our room, I realized one of our room keys was in the stolen bag. I called the front desk and apologized for losing it (along with the cool beach bag provided in our room). The desk agent seemed genuinely concerned about our misfortune and assured me that new beach bags would be provided by housekeeping and he would disable our old room keys and issue new ones.

Something unusual about this hotel: they use *real metal keys*, not plastic cards. But they are electronically encoded. When I got downstairs, our new keys were ready.

I found Bob at the bar and told him that he'd have to surrender the old key. Later, on passing the front desk, he deposited it in the box and we went back to our room. When we opened the door, we were greeted with a beautiful, large canvas beach bag holding two huge, plush beach towels. It was a consolation gift from the hotel. How nice!

Next day, we turned in the burgled Dodge Charger for a Chevy Malibu. The rest of our time in Hawaii went without a hitch. But we watched the weather reports and saw what was heading our way back home. Our timing appeared to be perfect. By the time our plane was scheduled to land back in Newark on Sunday, the freak Halloween snowstorm would be well away, the highways would be clear and the skies would be sunny. There were no delays. Our flight would leave on time and arrive early. Oh, well. This was one time I'd have been happy for a delay.

I received a wake-up call from one of the nurses at Mom's group home: there was no power at *five* of their facilities, including Montville. Mom was going to be moved to Ramsey, one of the locations with power. She was okay, but would have to double up for a while.

Upon landing in Newark, I turned my cellphone on and got a message from our pet sitter. Her phones were not working, so she was using her daughter's cell. I got every few words. "Limbs and branches." "No power." "Fed the cats extra." Huh boy.

Well, no use crying about it. We were safely on the ground. We were reunited with all our bags, and my car was waiting in Long Term Parking. I have a VW Beetle, and snow tends to slide off its rounded form, and I did have a scraper in the trunk.

The roads were clear and I got us home pretty quickly. We saw a lot of downed trees along the way, but as we approached Ringwood, it got worse. Bob called the Skyline Traffic Information Line, and the main artery home was closed. I took the alternate.

Our block was hit hard. Our house appeared to be intact, but there were huge branches down everywhere and saplings hanging onto our back room and hot tub. The driveway sported a ten-inch layer of wet snow, which is immovable by snow blower and impassible by VW Bug. The power was out, so I had to wade through the snow and debris in my new sneakers, up into the house to open the garage from inside and liberate our shovels. All that time in transit, added to the six-hour time difference, had us weary as it was. But the only way inside was to dig. So we sucked it up and dug.

Bob was alarmed by how heavy some of the fallen limbs were and did his best to clear the drive. We both shoveled as neighbors slowed in their vehicles to welcome us home, share a few words and get going to wherever they were heading following this latest natural disaster.

Eventually, we got the driveway clear so we could get the car into the garage and unload our bags. I wouldn't be doing laundry anytime soon.

None of the electrical comforts of home worked, but we did have a natural gas fireplace, so we could heat the main living area. The kitchen stove could be lit with a match. I had enough juice in my laptop batteries to keep my phone charged and at least keep some contact with the outside world. We had candles for light and cat food for the cats. Upon closer inspection, our home was not damaged. We simply got left in a holding pattern, waiting to get back to "normal" as the pain of leaving our island paradise clung to our tanned, chilled bodies.

By Monday evening at 9 p.m., our power was restored. I raced around the house turning the internet back on and resetting things. In short order, we realized just how truly lucky we were. Many of our neighbors would wait many more days for their electricity to return. My car, which would have been demolished by falling limbs had we left it in its usual spot and opted to take a cab to the airport, was safe and intact inside the garage. Mom was safe in Ramsey. And we were finally home on the other side of limbo.

CHAPTER 37:
REFLECTIONS ON THE YEAR

December 31, 2011

After a very busy weekend, which included a visit with Mom, I'm confronted with another holiday season. I do love this time of year. I don't mind the cold; I enjoy brisk walks, and I love the lights and holiday decorations. I'm filled with anticipation and excitement at seeing friends, having some laughs, and finding the right gifts for people I love. It's my kind of season.

This time last year, Mom had her first major psychotic break. I won't dwell upon the particulars; they were adequately documented (see Chapter 6). But what a year it's been.

Now that Mom is ensconced in Ramsey, I have the luxury of being able to think about other things. I visit her once a week, and I usually leave with a list of things she needs and thoughts about what I can do to keep her as comfortable as possible. It gets trickier, because so much of what she experiences these days is her questionable version of reality.

Mom thinks she has a job at the home. It mostly involves keeping the other residents in line, as she tells it. She complained that they kept her up until after three in the morning that Saturday evening with all those poor people stranded and unable to get on the boat back home. (Yes, the boats are back.) The noise from the street, the railroad (there is a train

that runs through Ramsey; that's real), and the toots of the
boat whistles (no water in Ramsey except for a few ponds
and small lakes) make it difficult for her to sleep. I offered to
buy her ear plugs (her hearing is eerily acute for someone her
age), but she declined.

She wants a phone. The staff isn't responsive enough. She
feels the need to be able to call me at will. I told her it would
cost about sixty dollars a month for a phone in her room.
In the past that would have stopped her cold; this time she
wasn't bothered by that expense. What about a cellphone?
She thought she might try it. Again.

Now, of course, I've been down this road with her before.
She couldn't work the simplest cellphone when she was more
lucid. Now, she'd lose it before it even got charged up. And if
she *could* manage to use the phone, what would she do with
it? Call me at all hours to complain about the crowds of people in her room waiting for the boat ride home?

I researched walkie-talkies, but those would require the
procurement of a license to traverse more than two miles
(we're about eight miles apart as the crow flies). I even
researched a converter that would allow her to use a cell line
like a land line.

The further I dug, the closer I came to the realization
that I was wasting time trying to answer a rhetorical question. Mom doesn't need a phone any more than she needs a
passport. She travels great distances in her imagination all the
time with no documentation. She often tells me she "tried to
call" me and couldn't reach me. What she needs is what she
has: a comfortable, safe place to live where she's given attention, affection, and regular visits from her family.

Happy Holidays folks, and a *healthy* New Year. Without
your health, nothing else matters.

CHAPTER 38:
RIDING IT OUT

January 17, 2012

"Oh, I'm so surprised I found you at home! I hate to bother you, but I need a ride. Can you come get me?"

Mom's calls often start this way. She has someone at the home call me on my cell (so I could theoretically be anywhere; she just assumes I'm "home") because she's certain she's been out on a merry jaunt and can't find transportation back to wherever it is she's supposed to be. And there are always others with her, stuck in the same predicament.

"Sure, Mom. It's okay. If you need me, I'll come. How are you feeling? Are you still having to go to the bathroom a lot?'

"It's better, but I'm still going more than usual."

"Okay. Can I talk to one of the girls?"

I get one of the nurses on the line. Mom has another urinary tract infection and she's being treated with antibiotics, and encouraged to drink lots of water (which explains the excessive peeing). I always delve a little further to try to get a handle on what's *really* troubling her when she seems agitated. Since last summer's misadventures, I'm on guard for any potential red flags.

According to the nurse, she's been calm and fine all day. Mom likes to follow her favorites around and watch them work. She did this with me too. Watching others work tires her out.

Fast forward a week and I have still not seen Mom. I've been sick. Today I have a low-grade fever. A sore throat over the weekend convinced me to take it easy and rest, but it wasn't enough. Now I'm coughing and achy. I need to see a medical doctor. But I already have an appointment with my eye doctor in Ramsey, and a visit with Mom is pending. I'm on the fence about it though. I don't want to get anyone else sick, especially not a houseful of vulnerable elders.

I'm also concerned about the "Selma" incident.

Last week, while I was on another call, an old friend of my parents, Selma,[22] called. She had tried to call Mom at the place in Wayne (from whence Mom had made a hasty exit in July). I told her where Mom was and gave her the new number, assuring her that Mom would certainly still remember her. Within the hour, one of the nurses called me to ask "Who's Selma?" I told her it was okay, she was an old friend of Mom's. The nurse understood, but told me Mom didn't remember her and didn't want to talk to her. I was shocked. Selma had gone to kindergarten with my father. Mom had known her for years. I expected short-term memory loss, but this?

I gave the nurse a few key prompts to jog Mom's memory about this old friend and hoped she'd remember. Of all the people Mom might forget, I didn't think Selma would be one of them.

Apparently, in the elder care game, this happens a lot and the nurse handled it well. She told Selma that Mom was napping and would call back later.

As I waited for a callback from my doctor, I decided to check back with the home. The nurse I'd spoken to over the "Selma" situation picked up. How did that go? Based on the

---

[22] Not her real name.

prompts I'd given, Mom did remember and had a lovely conversation with Selma. When she got off the phone, Mom continued to share the retrieved flood of memories with the kind nurse. I felt better.

Then I explained that I was sick and didn't want to infect Mom or anyone else there. I also didn't want to panic Mom; in her condition, a sneeze can turn into a coma faster than you can say "Gesundheit." (Last summer, when she was at the psychiatric hospital, she welled up when she saw me because she had been convinced I'd been in a serious accident.) The nurse assured me that maintaining a distance would be wise under the circumstances and she'd let Mom know of my condition should she ask. Boy, am I glad I called.

Next, I called the eye doctor to reschedule. They too were grateful I'd decided to keep my germs to myself. By next Monday, I should be fine (or at least no longer contagious).

All I have left is the council meeting tonight at 8 p.m. One of my jobs is to air, record, and schedule rebroadcasts of our town's governing body in action. For that, I am sequestered in a room by myself. I will be seeing my doctor this afternoon and hope to have some cough medicine to help me through it. Even if I don't have physical contact with anyone, the microphones could pick up my hacking through the walls. And no one else knows how to do this job.

This is my body telling me to rest, slow down, stop pushing. Okay, body, you win. Let's ride this out and evict these stupid germs. Meanwhile, tell Selma I'm taking a nap.

CHAPTER 39:
SUBJECT TO INTERPRETATION

February 4, 2012

My mom used to tell stories about my precociousness as a child. She claims that I started singing the refrain to *Old MacDonald* (E-I-E-I-O) at seven months of age. She was thrilled when I was finally able to let her know, by pointing and crying, rather than just crying, that I had an earache. At last, she could help me without trying to guess the cause of my distress.

These days, Mom often acts the role of my crying baby. Her pleas for help, her odd comments, the apparently unfounded complaints, all having some basis in a shared reality that I am required to decipher. Is someone *really* stealing her stuff? Does she actually need a ride somewhere? Is her agitation coming from her established conditions, or is something new and more sinister brewing?

My brother called last week to relate a call he received from Mom asking for a ride home. I explained that this was part of her illness and that she was confused about where she was. It's always best to reassure her, tell her you love her, and you'll see her soon. And then ask to speak to whomever dialed the phone. They can usually confirm what's going on. Just be glad she still knows you.

On a recent weekend, Bob and I took Mom out for brunch. Our birthdays are two days apart, so we figured a little joint celebration was in order. I brought Mom earrings I had been keeping for her and a birthday card I'd received from a friend of hers.

We had a nice meal and brought Mom back to the home. A guy who sings and plays guitar for the residents was entertaining the gals and Mom was excited. Bob wasn't feeling well and was waiting for me in the car. I sat Mom down in the living room, where she was honored with a rousing chorus of *Happy Birthday*, and I ran up to her room to put away her earrings and her birthday card.

As I prepared to leave, I told Mom where I put her stuff, kissed her, told her I'd be back tomorrow, and went to join my husband in the car.

Later, my cellphone rang. It was Mom. "What did you want me to remember?"

I told her that I left the birthday card from her friend on her dresser and put the little pouch holding her earrings in the top drawer. She searched where I suggested and found the items.

"Oh wonderful! I'm so glad I can still talk to you and ask you about things I need to remember."

You and me both, Mom. I'll always try to figure out where it hurts. I'm just so glad you're still able to point.

CHAPTER 40:
TIME TO KILL THE CAT

March 15, 2012

I've always been more of a dog person, but Bob loves cats. Once you get started with one type of pet, it's hard to switch. In my experience, cats tend to do better in pairs. They keep each other company while you're running around away from the house. They groom each other and give each other exercise and comfort. If one dies, the other tends to mourn and generally appreciates a new companion.

Back when Mom was living with us in 2010, we had two cats: Grady, the elder gray tiger, and Max, the younger tuxedo cat. They got along pretty well despite their age difference, but Grady, as he aged and became enfeebled, became impatient with young Max. Grady succumbed to cancer at sixteen. We were grateful that Grady managed to stay functional until after Mom returned to Florida so she didn't have to witness his coup de grace.

Knowing that the mass twisting his body was an inoperable malignancy, Bob and I agreed that once Grady hit certain benchmarks, it would be time. If he stopped eating or appeared to be in pain, we would end his suffering as soon as possible. As long as he had quality of life, we would spoil him and love him all we could. The day came when he would no longer eat. I made his final appointment.

We brought Grady to our vet, who assured us we were doing the right thing. Grady was contorted by a huge tumor. He was anemic. He'd had enough. We petted him and wept as the doctor administered his sweet release. His remains are buried in our yard under a headstone inscribed with "Grady – A Feline Success."

Sad as it was to lose him, this was a "good death." Grady had a good, long, happy run. We loved him dearly and still miss him, but it was clearly his time and we accepted it.

Max missed Grady. He would start up with me, initiating cat fights. I figured we'd eventually get him a playmate. Max was six and had enjoyed feline company all his life.

One of our neighbors asked us about taking in kittens *twice*. We eagerly said yes, but each time, she'd give away the kittens to others or decide to keep them for herself. So I decided to look at shelter kittens.

The local shelters post descriptions and pictures of their adoptees online. One caught my eye: "Kohl," a long-haired baby of five months. Could we go take a look?

Bob and I went to the shelter and looked at every cat they had. Lots of heartbreaking cuties were looking for homes. I asked about "Kohl." We were brought to his cage. When the door was opened, the kitten in question literally leapt into my arms. I was on the hook. This dark brown, long-haired beauty was coming home with us.

Problems soon followed. Being locked up in "juvey" for five months, this kitten was damaged. Skittish, plagued with chronic diarrhea, and fearful of being handled for drug administration, he was a tough case. He did like music and rolled around on Bob's amplifier as he played his bass. He also watched TV and tried to catch birds and other critters he saw on the big screen. He even proved to be a good hunter, having killed a baby mole and left it in our bedroom, jammed under the baseboard heating register. And he would cuddle with me, but only when I was sleeping, presumably so I couldn't do anything to hurt him.

We renamed him "Cody" (a nod to his obvious enjoyment of music, inspired by the term "Coda") and tried to help him settle into life with us.

Mom saw him a couple of times before she moved to assisted living. She was impatient to see the kitty, but he wasn't cooperative. When she'd get near, he would hide. She did comment that his tail looked like a "bottle brush."

Rather than acclimate to being handled and cared-for, Cody became more skittish. He'd hiss, scream, and squirm away when I tried to give him any kind of medicine. He would only allow brushing where he didn't need it. He looked like no one cared for him because no one could. It was maddening.

Eventually, he developed gingivitis. We'd had another cat with chronic gingivitis: Marty. He had been a sweet, loving cat who'd let me do anything to him. We had taken Marty in when he was about five months old (he was an outdoor stray) and he fit right in with two other cats in the household (one of whom was Grady). I gave him antibiotic drops almost daily for most of his nine years. He even allowed me to brush his grotty gums (which was like trying to mop a dirt floor). Eventually, he developed kidney failure from the toxins in his gums. All things considered, he had great quality of life. He was worth every moment, every cent of care he required. He returned our love many times over and I still miss him eight years after his departure.

But Cody was a completely different story. The older and stronger he got, the harder it was to do anything for him. Bringing him to the vet for his checkups and shots was a two-day process. Figuring out how to get him in the box and transport him safely to and from the vet was a lot of work. In fact, he pooped himself once inside the box, and then busted out of the cardboard carrier after being placed in the car. During one checkup visit, his gingivitis was diagnosed. I asked the vet for tranquilizers to give him to see if I could calm him down to care for him further.

I managed to get a pill down his throat one time. It made him a little wobbly, but no easier to grab, hold, or manage. I tried putting the antibiotic in his food. He wouldn't touch it. It was becoming obvious that this was one sick kitty who would only get worse.

Cody started to shriek for no apparent reason. He'd try to eat and then scream. Clearly, his mouth was sore. He wasn't eating much. Bob and I compared notes.

Meanwhile, Max had developed health problems. First, he was vomiting almost daily. Then he was losing hair on his thighs. I brought him to the vet and he was given cortisone shots, the idea being that he might have food allergies.

The vomiting stopped, but Max lost weight at an alarming rate. He went from sixteen pounds to 11.5. He screamed for food constantly and continued losing weight. He was also thirsty and peeing a lot. He developed a cough too.

Max had become diabetic and required injections of insulin twice a day. We dreaded this at first, but Max accepted his treatment gracefully, barely taking notice of the thin needles delivering his insulin as he ate. He got better. He gained weight. The drinking and peeing slowed and went back to healthy levels. I took him to the vet weekly to monitor his blood glucose levels and titrate his insulin doses.

During one visit to the vet, I voiced my concerns about Cody and my inability to treat him. She knew how hard I tried. I was clearly a caring pet owner. I told her what I'd been rolling around in my head; that maybe it was time to put Cody out of his and our misery. She kindly told me that what I was thinking was not a bad thing. Some pets are simply not meant for this world.

I told Bob. He was more than supportive. He blamed Cody for Max's deterioration. We decided we'd bring him in on a Saturday so Bob could help corral Cody and keep the plan on track.

We plotted Cody's capture and managed to get him into a cardboard carrier. We actually had to put that box inside a kennel with metal bars in order to get him to the vet. He busted out of the box while inside the kennel, but the kennel contained him.

We arrived at the vet's office and I informed the receptionist that Cody had pooped in the box and maybe should be sequestered from the waiting room. We were ushered directly into an exam room to wait for the vet.

A different doctor attended to Cody. He extracted him from the kennel and removed the poop, shaving the turds sticking to his long, unkempt hair away and checking him over. Yes, his gums were mighty inflamed. They could pull all his teeth, or give him steroids. We'd have to give him drugs at home, bring him back and...

I started to sob as I once again explained the trouble we'd had trying to care for this poor damaged animal. It wasn't like we could put him up for adoption by anyone else. And it wasn't as if we hadn't tried every other reasonable option.

He understood. He asked a few questions, had us sign some papers, and brought Cody to another room to administer his last treatment. He said we'd feel crummy for a few days, but he agreed we were doing the right thing.

Max improved almost immediately. He'd been putting weight back on, but now he was back in our laps, sleeping with us, playing with us, and acting the way he used to a year ago. I couldn't believe how much he'd changed and how quickly he'd changed back. Now I felt bad for putting Max through all this trauma. But I was glad he wasn't suffering any longer, and thrilled that we weren't either.

We tried so hard to do all the right things. In the end, we had to recognize the true problem and eliminate it for the greater good. Sometimes, you have to do the hard thing. If I had to put down one sad creature to save the life of our cherished pet, I'm okay with the choice. Max is once again thriving, happy and healthy. He may even regain the ability to make his own insulin.[23] It's never an option to take lightly, but sometimes, you just have to kill the cat.

---

[23] Sadly, that was not to be. In July of 2016, at age twelve, Max was diagnosed with metastatic cancer and we had to put him to sleep as well. That was a terrible, sudden shock.

CHAPTER 41:
REPEAT THAT, PLEASE

March 25, 2012

The definition of insanity is repeating the same action and expecting a different result. In my role as caregiver to both my mother and my cat, I visit that edge on a regular basis.

My cat, Max, as previously noted, has diabetes and must be fed on a schedule. He must also be injected with insulin twice a day, every twelve hours. We've learned that "shooting the bat,"[24] as we've come to call it, is easier when he's preoccupied with eating, which also keeps his blood glucose on an even keel. He gets Fancy Feast, which he usually loves, and prescription crunchies. When he was sick and malnourished from the diabetes, his appetite was alarming. He'd suck down two cans in a sitting (and reject the dry food he used to love). He'd barely acknowledge the thin needle delivering his medication. But now that he's back to a good weight (about fourteen pounds), he still cries for food after he's been fed. He'll eat a few bites, walk away and clean himself, then forget

---

[24] One of Max's nicknames is "Bat Boy," due to his cartoonish looks (he's a not-quite-symmetrical tuxedo cat) and distinctive black mask. And "shoot the bat" sounds so much less ominous than "inject with insulin."

there's food in his dish. I will then walk him back to his still-full dish, but he continues to cry. I tried a number of things to get him to dig in, but I found an answer, quite by accident. He needs to be placed at 9 o'clock to his food dish, with his left shoulder to the wall, and then he will eat. Bizarre but true. If he's at 6 o'clock to the dish, it might as well be empty.

I go through similar gyrations with Mom. A couple of weeks ago, after Bob and I took her out for lunch, I schlepped her packed suitcase back up to her room (she often packs her suitcase, thinking my brother or I will be taking her else-where) and noticed that all her photo albums were wrapped in brown plastic bags. I asked her why she did this, and she insisted that the place was closing and she was going to have to move. I reassured her that was not the case and suggested she unpack her things. It would give her something to do. I told her Bob and I were going away the next weekend to see our nieces, but I'd see her soon after that.

During the following week, I got a call from an RN hired by Mom's long-term care insurer. They wanted her re-evalu-ated. Would that be okay? I told the nurse I would be happy to arrange it and meet her there. I wanted to see how Mom was doing through professional assessment standards and I think she's a little less stressed by the procedure if I'm there to observe and support her.

On the appointed day, the nurse was running late, but I figured I'd spend a little more quality time with Mom. Up in her room, not only was the stuff still packed in bags from last time, she had packed even *more* stuff. And people were steal-ing her underwear and makeup! No, Mom, they're packed in your luggage and in brown plastic bags. I unpacked every-thing, hanging some of her clothes, putting other items in her dresser drawers, showing them to her to reassure her, once again, that her things were still there, still safe, and now being stored and organized for her use. I shuffled the items in her closet, putting her slacks in one section, blouses in another, coat and jackets on the far right.

"All that work," Mom sighed. (Whether she meant her work or my work, I'll never know for sure.)

This was second nature to me at this point. I must have done this exercise in the various places she's lived at least twenty times (including her time at my house). This time, I was doing it so I could get a handle on what things she might truly need. I know the next time I see her, everything will be tossed around, if not packed, yet again. But at least I know she's still got hair spray, soap, toothpaste, and Poise pads (they apparently make great packing material).

After her interview with the nurse, I sat with Mom in the main living area and we chatted. Mom said something about having recently had dinner with Dad.

"Really? When was this?"

"I get confused between Daddy and the one who came after him."

Me too, Mom. There was no one after Daddy. You made up some other fellow in your head, someone you've never been able to name. Someone you think you were married to, who had a hostile family and a wandering eye. His story is fascinating, but he doesn't exist, at least not in my world.

Then she started enumerating things she needs. Knee highs, in white.

"Socks? No problem."

"And underwear."

"I can get you more. Did you try on the new panties we bought?"

"Yeah. I need a different size."

"Were they too small or too big?"

"Uh, I don't know. You know that one stole my underwear. But I got even with her. I took one of her blouses."

Her. They. Him. Stolen. Oy.

Then Mom says, "I know it's a pipe dream, but I'm thinking I might need a new bathing suit. The ones I have are old and they, you know…"

"The elastic goes bad."

"Yeah."

"Okay, we'll have to go to a department store and you'll have to try some on."

"Yeah, okay. I'm thinking it's also time to see someone about my face again."

"You want another face-lift? That's kind of expensive, Ma. And you might not be strong enough to deal with it. You don't heal that well."

"Well, if I get a twinkle in my eye…"

"Yeah, okay, we'll see."

When she'd gone for her "Lifestyle Lift" back in 2007, my brother was thrilled (he's a fan of modern plastic surgical techniques). I was delighted because she was doing something life-affirming and positive for herself. Now, she lives in a home where the only male is a twenty-six-year-old healthcare aide. But in her head, she could be back in Florida flirting with some spry guy with the bat of an eyelash.

And here I sit, recording my musings on the meaning of caregiving, praying that I am never on the receiving end, hoping that my perspective will be of value to others and wishing that my cat would stop screaming at me for food, at least until the next "bat bell" rings.[25]

Shriek. Feed. Shriek. Redirect.

Pack. Unpack. Reorganize. Placate.

I'm tired. But I'm not going to the funny farm. Not just yet, anyway. Because unlike my charges, I am well aware that the results will continue to be pretty much the same no matter how many times the actions are repeated.

---

[25] I set reminders on my iPhone so we'll remember to deliver Max's food and insulin on time. These alarms have come to be known as the "Bat Bell." And when Max arrives in my bedroom at 7:30 a.m. to scream for his breakfast, that too is known as the "Bat Bell."

CHAPTER 42:
DESIGNER GENES

May 18, 2012

My interest in dementia has led me to a variety of resources, including the Alzheimer's Association. They've provided support and guidance throughout my journey with my mother. I receive a newsletter from the Greater New Jersey chapter, and recently I found an interesting article about dementia research in the issue from Spring 2012.

In the middle of the state of New Jersey there is a Memory Enhancement Center where a study exploring the genetic risk of developing Alzheimer's is being conducted. As the child of someone who clearly has dementia, I have already pondered the obvious questions: "what if this happens to me?" or "will this happen to me?" My mother may not have Alzheimer's (we'll know after she passes)[26] but her older sister did die from it. In addition, my mother's mother had "organic brain disease" indicated as a contributing cause of

---

[26] Mom had Alzheimer's disease. It was confirmed by analysis of her brain as part of an Alzheimer's study conducted by Mount Sinai. I enrolled Mom through Trial Match. The data derived from studying my mother's brain will contribute to finding a cure.

her death in 1980. My Grandma Nettie had suffered speech aphasia several years before she died, finding it difficult to speak English, reverting to her native Yiddish when last I saw her alive. With the genetic cards apparently stacked against me, at least on my mother's side, I contacted the folks running the study. An ideal candidate, I really wanted to know if I had the genetic predisposition.

Now, let me clear up a few things:

Having the suspicious gene does *not* mean a person will definitely develop Alzheimer's. What it does mean is that the likelihood that they will develop Alzheimer's is higher than for those who don't have the gene. And conversely, not having the gene doesn't let you completely off the hook either. You just have better odds in favor of holding on to your faculties as you age when managing other risk factors, like lifestyle.

The results of the genetic test may *not* be shared with your insurance company. This is why we have privacy laws in this country. Keep it to yourself and your carrier will never know.

The test does not hurt. You don't even need to give blood; the inside of your cheek can be swabbed to derive the necessary material to test your DNA for the gene.

Since I had to be in New Brunswick for a conference the first week in May, I contacted these folks and offered myself up for testing.

First, they did a cognitive test. I am very familiar with these, as I have been with Mom on the numerous occasions she was subjected to them.

What's today's date?
Who is the president?
Remember three words: "apple," "table," "penny."
Please write down any sentence that comes to mind.
"I ate the apple and put a penny on the table."

Copy a line drawing of two intersecting pentagrams.
Can you remember the three words? Yep: apple, table, penny.

I scored twenty-nine out of thirty because I exaggerated the way the pentagrams were drawn on the test. I showed the tester how the intersections were not clean (as a graphic artist, I am a stickler for precision), and told him he owed me half a point.

Then he swabbed my cheeks and told me he'd call with the results. It could be two days or two weeks.

Following some delays, I finally received word: *I don't have the gene!* Yippee!

Again, this is no guarantee, but my odds of aging without dementia just took a 20 percent uptick. Add healthy lifestyle and the odds continue to improve.

If you are the child of someone with dementia, you might want to consider participating in a study. We are the generation that could well escape the fate of our parents. But research must be done and subjects are needed.

Of course, you may not want to know. Ignorance may be bliss, for a while. And you may be so burdened with your loved one's care that you might not have the time. But consider it. You may be lucky, like me. You may be unlucky. Either way, you'll have one of many answers to a nagging question and you'll be helping researchers find the answers to the bigger questions. Hopefully, one day the answer will be "Yes! We *have* found a cure for Alzheimer's!"

If you want to explore trials that are currently being conducted, I encourage you to check out "Trial Match" through the Alzheimer's Association's website, alz.org. You have nothing to lose. You may even find a cutting-edge treatment for your loved one. Whatever you decide, I wish you well and hope you find the answers you need.

CHAPTER 43:
WAIT UNTIL MORNING

June 22, 2012

As the sun goes down, up goes the angst.

This is what I must remember: tonight's panic will be forgotten tomorrow. That's how this nasty business works.

Lately, Mom's sundowning behaviors have been more aggressive, leading the staff at the home to call me to see if I can calm her down. She grabs for the door and tries to run away. She hasn't tried anything like this since last summer, when she still lived at the ALF and had to be watched by additional hired guardians.

The staff knows I'm okay with receiving these calls. If I can soothe her by phone and keep them from having to give her additional meds, I'm glad to do it. Many other families reject such calls. I prefer to know what's going on and I do what I can.

It tends to be exhausting, though. Trying to parse what bee got into Mom's bonnet isn't easy, especially as her language skills are declining, and her ability to report on the myriad fleeting thoughts fluttering about her neural net often eludes her. So I try to sift through the quicksand for something I can grab hold of and manage.

On this particular Monday afternoon, Mom was sure the place was being evacuated and she had to get out of there. She didn't want to bother me, but she didn't know where she'd be able to lay her head down come the evening.

I told Mom I would make phone calls to ensure that she could stay put. I would have Julia Roberts get involved if necessary.

"Well, that's fine for you to say, but I need some assurance."

"Okay, Mom, I can come see you tomorrow."

"When? What time?"

"I can come in the morning, Ma. I'll see you tomorrow morning."

Then I asked to speak to the gal who dialed the phone. This was one of the more senior people who manages the facilities. Mom handed the phone back to her.

"Mom thinks the place is closing. Can you please reassure her? I'll come by tomorrow, but in the meantime..."

"That's what was upsetting her? No problem, I'll let her know she's safe."

Thanking her, I hung up and reviewed my schedule for Tuesday. There was nothing that couldn't wait, so I sent emails and rescheduled things. I could run some other errands too.

Monday is my yoga night. I look forward to the class. The regulars are all dear women with great energy, and the instructor is awesome, intuitive, and nurturing. I make a point of getting there every week.

Sure enough, our instructor keyed in on the vibe in the room. Dealing with my mother really does deplete me. Anticipating seeing her saps my strength like nothing else.

One pose in this practice was one I'd never formally tried before, although it's kind of natural for me to arrange my body in that way without knowing its name: The Turtle. Seated on the floor, bending at the waist and wrapping your legs over your arms helps you to fold forward in half, and feel protected by your limbs around your torso. I got deep into it. I felt the tension melt. I went meditative. I completely related to the spirit of the pose.

Back when Mom still lived with us, I had tried to explain my family dynamic to my husband. When I was a child, my mother leaned on me for support and friendship. She was never a social person. The older I got, the more I needed to retreat from her. I'd hide in my room and immerse myself in my music, my art, television, radio, books. My father referred to me as "The Hermit." This was self-preservation. This was my respite from my mother's neediness, neurosis, and demands.

Living with her once again in adulthood, the remnants of the old dynamic remained, but I couldn't just run away now; that could be dangerous in her compromised state. No matter how crazy she made me, I would have to stick it out and try to cope. Sometimes, I'd get nasty with her, and Bob would defend her and chastise me. He couldn't know how tough this was for me. He hadn't known me as child and tended to simplify the situation as he understood it.

So now I have the luxury of long periods of respite. But I don't get to stay away. I still have to manage Mom's care, visit her, talk to her, keep her feeling that she's safe.

So on Tuesday, I got an early start and ran my errands, all the while buttressing myself for my visit to Mom. I entered the home and was greeted by one of the caretakers.

"She's right in there."

Good morning, Sunshine!

Mom was dressed and seated at one of the tables, receiving a manicure from one of the aides. She was quite calm and chatted amiably with the gal. She looked up at me, clearly pleased and a little surprised. I kissed her and sat down.

"What brings you here?"

"I told you I'd come see you this morning."

"Oh? Well, that's nice. Where's Bobby?"

Clearly, she did not remember that we'd spoken the evening before. But she did remember the fiancé of the gal who painted her fingernails and that they were soon to be married. Amazing.

I stayed and chatted a while. Her conversation meandered. She was disappointed at not being able to get Herby on the phone, nor the other one (her invented newer husband) either. I tried to follow what she was saying, but I would get lost in her confusion, and I guess the fatigue showed on my face. She asked if there was something I could take to perk myself up. I told her it was a little stuffy in there for me and I'd wake up when I got outside. When I felt like she was content, I rose to leave. She walked me to the door, I kissed her goodbye, and off I went. No unpleasantness. No pleading. No acrimony. No lunge for freedom.

Back home, I felt quite relieved and was able to resume business activities. I felt better, lighter, productive.

Around 5:30 p.m., just as my husband was arriving home from work, my phone rang. The caller ID displayed Mom's number. Huh-boy.

One of the aides was on the phone. Mom was freaking out. Again.

I inhaled and told her, "I was just there this morning."

"I didn't know that. But you know, I come in at 3. She's trying to leave again. And I don't want to give her drugs if I don't have to."

"Of course. Let me talk to her."

Anticipating the usual "sky is falling," "home is closing," "need a ride out of here" lines of hysteria, I was surprised when Mom told me she was concerned about her Social Security paperwork. Was there something she had to sign? She couldn't find her ID (because I have all of it).

Later that same day...

"No, Mom. Not to worry. I took care of it. In fact, I went to Paterson to make sure all the paperwork was done properly." This was the truth. Several months ago, I had gone to the Social Security office in the county seat to fill out paperwork to become Mom's "Representative Payee." This enabled me to switch banks and have her Social Security checks direct deposited into a new account for her. I used that experience to formulate an explanation which calmed her right down. I told her she could call me anytime she had questions or needed anything. I told her I loved her and she said the same to me as we ended our session.

"I couldn't believe you were on the phone with her. Didn't you just see her this morning?" asked my incredulous husband as he kissed me hello.

Sure I did. But that was this morning. She's better in the morning. She had just recently had her morning meds and breakfast. Later in the day, the sun descends, the meds start to wear off, her blood sugar drops, her head fills up with uncontrollable thoughts, and the phone calls begin.

So another piece of the ever-changing puzzle falls into place. See her in the morning. Listen to her as necessary and reassure her in the evening. And make time to do The Turtle in between.

CHAPTER 44:
DELAYED REACTION

July 19, 2012

Recently, I was hit by an emotional bus. It came out of nowhere and blindsided me.

In truth, it came out of me. It had been buried, hidden, stomped down, and denied. But after inviting it to resurrect two days in a row, it reconstituted fully and hit me hard in the heart.

Last Tuesday, I had a meeting with another entrepreneurial woman. We had met a couple of years ago at a business women's group. We had talked about working together, but at the time, her needs and my strengths were not a perfect match, so we drifted off in our own respective directions. I stayed on her email list and followed her progress. I noticed that she had changed direction recently, and I reached out to see if there might be a new opportunity for us to work together. We met for lunch.

As we caught up, I mentioned my hellish year dealing with my mother's condition. I talked about the difficult situation surrounding the sale of my parents' Florida apartment and the disposal of their copious quantities of stuff; dealing with the remnants of their life; acknowledging the cost of their indulgences and lack of understanding of the consequences until it was way too late. I talked a lot about my quest for knowledge regarding health, fitness, and the food we eat. This woman is a fitness coach, so we had a lot in common on this front, and we agreed that the future likely held some mutually beneficial opportunities.

Wednesday, I had a telephone consultation with another entrepreneurial woman, a career coach. This woman helps Fortune 500 companies and small business owners to strategize growth. We talked about what I want to be when I grow up, and how I've grappled with this problem all my life. I'm good at a lot of things. I love to sing, take photos, draw, paint, design, write, make videos. I told her about my small business marketing concept, developing YouTube channels. She thought that was a winning idea.

Along the way, I mentioned my passion for health, nutrition, and educating people about these important topics. I told her about my failed business venture, where I had formed a video production company with two partners to promote Ayurvedic[27] principles to the American public. She asked me what kind of shape I was in.

I told her in no uncertain terms that I am in excellent health and had spent the last year prioritizing my own well-being. I started to relate the story of my trip to Florida to sell my parents' apartment. Suddenly, I connected with a torrent of feeling I had not permitted myself to experience before. The pain of dealing with the disposal of all my parents' personal effects, artwork, and accumulated detritus; the sadness of saying a final goodbye to the place where my folks

---

[27] Ayurveda is a holistic school of Indian medicine focused on health through diet and exercise (yoga).

had spent the happiest time of their lives; the realization that all of that was now officially gone forever.

Tears filled my eyes and I fought to keep talking through my sobs. The coach was understanding and she handled it well. But I was more than a little surprised at my delayed reaction. *I thought I had dealt with this.* I thought I was done. I thought I was moving on and growing up. But there was clearly a whole lot of pain I had not processed that was just now bubbling to the surface, demanding to be felt.

We concluded the session on a positive note and I told the counselor I would pursue the idea and try to gain some clarity on how to proceed with it. I would also think about engaging her professionally to help me formulate a plan to carry the idea forward.

For the rest of the day, I felt terribly blue. Once I had taken care of as much business as I could handle, I made a point of doing a demanding workout. At this stage in my journey, it usually makes me feel better.

Still fighting profound sadness and not knowing what else to do with it, I began to write.

I couldn't help but think of my father, who could not cry when he'd lost his first child at the age of eighteen months to meningitis. Only when he lost his mind in his seventies did he begin to experience that long-denied sorrow. He allowed himself to recall Andy and cry for him at long last, fifty-plus years after the fact. He had to lose his ego to allow his soul to express his terrible grief.

And now I get my turn. Again.

Now that the tasks surrounding the dissolution of my parents' material life are passed, I am faced with finally grieving that loss. Just as I began grieving the loss of my father a

year before his body passed away. I lost the man and friend
my father had been long before his physical death.

No wonder I'm so fucking sad. I've lost so much, and
having been in crisis mode for such a long period, I had kept
the grief at bay. I suppose I should be grateful for having had
so much to lose in the first place. Or maybe I have the right
to have myself a good cry and hope I feel better tomorrow.
Boy, this grown-up stuff sucks.

CHAPTER 45:
LONG-TERM CARELESSNESS

July 26, 2012

In the process of caregiving, one thing that simply can't be overlooked is dealing with insurance companies. It's a hideous part of the role one must play. The hoops one must jump through, the forms one must fill out, the phone calls and the aggravation of dealing with entities whose prime directive is to deny first, ask questions later, is daunting, exhausting, and just plain evil.

I give thanks to my father regularly for having had the foresight to buy a long-term care policy for himself and Mom while they were still healthy enough to qualify. In addition, Dad left assets that help me bridge the gap when the insurance companies play their games and stop the flow of payments for whatever inane reason they concoct. But I fight for what's ours and succeed to whatever degree I can. I seem to be losing ground, however, because the cards are stacked in favor of these well-financed, labyrinthine bureaucracies, supported in part by our legislators who enable these entities to operate in this deplorable fashion.

My mother's policy was with the leading player in the long-term care insurance[28] marketplace (at the time). Truth be told, no insurers want this piece of business any longer. It's a loser. On a long enough timeline, odds are every insured party will become sick and will require some long-term care. Ironically, my father utilized almost none of his benefits, although I did open a claim and it was deemed valid. The trajectory of his illness was so quick in terms of his policy, he died before the "elimination period" for care in a facility had concluded, so we got hung paying all his expenses at assisted living. This included medication delivery, which we ordered the night before he died. The facility took our money for the drugs and the service which were *never used* and refused to refund any money after Dad passed away.

I opened Mom's claim when she started hallucinating in December 2010. Knowing how the insurance worked, I started with hiring in-home caregivers. They prefer you start this way. It's more cost-effective and helps you cope with your infirmity as you ride out the "elimination period." After one hundred days of in-home care, they would, if you jumped through all the right hoops and demonstrate that your loved one is truly in need of assistance with three out of five activities of daily living,[29] pay up to 125 dollars per day for assisted living. So while ALF facilities charge monthly, Mom's policy

---

[28] The company in question has since ceased the sale of new long-term care insurance policies, but continues to service in-force policies.

[29] Activities of Daily Living include going to the bathroom, transferring (functional mobility), self-feeding, dressing, and bathing. Cognitive impairment trumps all these, as patients who are afflicted have problems with all the ADLs to varying degrees through the course of their deterioration.

would pay 125 dollars per day, and our monthly reimbursements vary depending on how many days there are in a given month. That's *if* they agree there's a need and the facility chosen adequately fills the prescribed "plan of care."

Well, Mom definitely had needs which have been documented by a number of professionals and institutions. But with each new need and change of venue, I must document each one, every facility and its appropriateness for Mom's care, whether the LTC carrier is asked to pay for it or not. When medically necessary, as with Mom's UTIs and her falls, she has had to go to hospitals and rehab facilities. Those visits are paid for in part by her medical insurance (with varying co-pays borne by yours truly). Mom has a Medicare Advantage plan (which is actually an HMO).

The way this insurance works is, the insurance carrier gets paid by Social Security for Mom's Medicare policy premiums. They then administer her benefits. They don't charge anything extra for the insurance, but you must use their network of providers, which is pretty extensive, to receive the greatest benefit. Unfortunately, they're another ridiculous bureaucracy. When Mom fell down the stairs, she was taken to Valley Hospital's Emergency Room and then admitted. They denied her claim for the hospital stay ostensibly because the results of her initial tests were negative (no broken bones). The fact that she has a heart condition, was in screaming pain, and couldn't walk on her injured leg, and that her doctor wanted to run extensive tests to rule out significant underlying illnesses as having contributed to her fall, were not good enough reasons to admit her, at least not upon first submission. But they did approve physical therapy. Mom's doctor and advocates at the hospital will contest the denial and hopefully, no outrageous bills will come my way.

We'll see. There's nothing for me to do in this case but move forward and get Mom the treatment she needs right now.

Another thing I should mention for children of aging parents: go to an elder law attorney and get all their documentation squared away. Be designated your parents' Power of Attorney and Health Care Proxy so you can speak for and defend them when they can't do it for themselves. You should also have them draw up a Living Will (Advance Directive) which explains in detail how they want to be dealt with as regards resuscitation, intubation, and other potentially nasty life-prolonging procedures. And make sure you get professional advice on a Last Will and Testament to establish and honor their goals.

Meanwhile, the LTC carrier has proven to be in "hold up claims" mode. Two and a half months ago, the insurer realized that Mom had moved from one home in a system (which had passed all its criteria for appropriate care at the end of last summer's jump-through-the-hoops-fest) to another home in exactly the same system, with exactly the same qualifications, certifications and care provisions, back in October (this move was due to the freak snowstorm that knocked out the power in her facility). But the company obviously saw an opportunity to stop paying and took it.

I was confronted with two different "benefits analysts" who told me I didn't have to do anything but wait. They chased down documentation on the facilities she'd been to *last summer* which had long been paid and had not been submitted to them for payment. I had reported the chain of care to a previous benefits analyst so they would have a complete record of Mom's travels. Now they were using it as a further delay tactic. When I found this out, I called them on it and told them to drop the investigation, that these facilities had already been paid and had nothing to do with Mom's current care provision at the home in Ramsey.

Finally, after calling the LTC carrier a number of times, I learned the final obstacle was a "facility statement" that was pending from Mom's current group home. I called the group home, found out who was filling out the form, and got confirmation of its submission.

Then I called the LTC carrier and was promised a callback from "Jessica," the current benefits analyst, within twenty-four hours. The next day, I got the call and confirmation that all documentation had at last been received. When would I see the money?

An "off-cycle payment" could be requested "if you want." Yes, I want! But she could only release one payment at a time. I would get June's payment next week, and on the fifteenth of August, I would get the *July* payment only. What about August?

Well, they needed to wait for the entire month to elapse before they could pay me for August, to make sure Mom got her care from them. *What?*

All the preceding several months, I got charged for Mom's rent to be paid by the first of the month *in advance*. Is there anyone in the world who isn't charged on the first of the month for the month they will occupy a place of residence?

I had gotten into the habit of faxing in the invoice to the LTC carrier when it would come in, usually a couple of weeks before it was due. So I received the August bill, due August 1, around July 15. I would fax it to the LTC carrier, pay the bill on August 1, and receive reimbursement on August 15. *Now* the insurer is telling me that going forward, I will have to wait for September 15 to be reimbursed for August.

Wow, what a racket! The company gets to hold on to *Mom's money* for an extra month, collecting whatever interest it can on that money while I burn through my father's assets paying for all of Mom's other expenses, which include prescription drugs (over two hundred dollars per month, and she's hit the donut hole by now; can't wait to see *that* bill), hair care, sundries, and various co-pays (including fifty dollars a day for her physical therapy, which her Medicare will only deliver at one of their network facilities). Oh yeah, and did I mention that Mom's rent at the group home went up 250 dollars a month for this year, all of which I must absorb? And continue to pay whether she stays there or not?

Add to that, the banks pay *nothing* to consumers in interest. Every time I see an offer for "high interest" of way under 1 percent on a savings account, I want to scream. Meanwhile, credit costs consumers 3, 4, 5 percent or more for mortgages, and in excess of 15 percent for credit cards, even more for department store credit interest. Why is this permitted?

Then there are other investment instruments. I can't even bear to look at these. Junk bonds. Active Diversified Portfolios. Managed Accounts. I'm grateful for the annuity I bought for Mom that earns 4 percent. Makes me feel like a freakin' genius. When I think about how my dad used to live off the interest from his investments back in the '90s, I can't believe what's happened.

To the insurance companies upon whom we must depend: please understand that we are people, just like the ones in your own families. The next time you deny a claim for someone like my mother, imagine for a moment, that she's *your* mother. How would *you* feel? How would *she* feel if she were faced with fighting this without a healthy advocate?

Folks, it's time to get big picture. Our system is seriously broken and it must be fixed, or those of us who remain *will* revolt, will rise up, and will reclaim control. It's just a matter of time. And numbers. I am the majority demographic in this country, and I will take advantage of every opportunity afforded me by sheer numbers. Be warned. I will not take this without fighting back.

And you will pay for my long-term care should I get sick, LTC carrier. My husband and I have a policy, and I will not allow it to lapse and I will get every penny owed us should either of us ever need long-term care. You are preparing me well for my future. I'm hip to your tricks and I will be ready for you.

CHAPTER 46:
DON'T GET OLD

August 6, 2012

Facebook has its uses. I've met a variety of people online over the years, and the ones I've never met in real life are often the most provocative. After all, the reason we "met" was that one of us somehow provoked the other to think about something in a different way than we had before.

On Sunday, one of my Facebook friends "liked" a status that was rather challenging. The post was about how this person had always hated old people and now found himself to be an old man. This triggered a flurry of responses, some reacting to the initial "ageist" nature of the post, others commiserating with the oncoming specter of one's decrepitude and demise. I was tempted to chime in, but the more I thought about it, the less I wanted to add my two cents to the lengthy thread. My philosophy in the case of Facebook comments is "brevity is the soul of wit," and if I can't be witty, I might as well blog.

Having cared for two aging parents has forced me to confront my own advancing age for some time now. In January, I turned fifty-four. Depending on your perspective, you might think I'm already ancient (if you're five) or just a child (if you're eighty-five). But the way things have gone in the past year, I'd be inclined to quote Bob Dylan: "I was so much older then, I'm younger than that now."

My husband, Bob, had a dear friend, Chris, who was the best man at our wedding in 1991. They had been best friends in high school, stayed in touch through letters when Bob was in the Navy, and continued to be close through young adulthood. I met Chris when he was twenty-seven (and I was twenty-eight). He had a dry sense of humor which he lubricated liberally with alcohol and weed. I distinctly remember his thirtieth birthday party: it was a depraved and drunken debauch that was clearly the last night of his youth. Immediately following that event, Chris got old. He never dated. He lived with his mother. He worked as a landscaper (a profession that allowed him to drink on the job). In time, Bob could no longer stand to witness his friend's slow, self-inflicted demise and they parted ways. By the time they reconciled, Chris had terminal cirrhosis. He died at forty-nine, an old and lonely man.

I met my father-in-law when he was fifty-nine. At his sixtieth birthday party, he turned old. He could not bear to acknowledge the inevitable change of the guard, that his children were succeeding him and were very capable of taking care of themselves and their families. His ego demanded that he retain absolute power as family monarch, which was, of course, impossible. Gradually, he pushed away everyone who cared about him, turned to drink, and died a lonely old man at seventy-four.

My mother is eight-three. She's been old for a very long time. I remember her using the expression "I'm too old for…" when she was still in her forties. Personal growth and introspection were never part of her makeup.

My father was different. He got a second chance at life when he was fifty-six. A double-bypass operation made him reassess his life and priorities. He and my mother began living it up and having fun together. They traveled. They bought a place on the Jersey shore and another in Florida. Dad bought his first computer at seventy-three (and he was my best student). He often joked about "the golden years" being a "crock of shit," but continued to grow as a human being, enthusiastically embracing life until he realized he was losing his mind (vascular dementia was at the top of his list of ailments) at seventy-five. Losing him was particularly hard, because he got old so damned fast. His body died at seventy-six.

Last year, after having cared for my mother for several years, much of it hands-on in my own home, I had become old. I had gained weight, gotten tired, sad, depressed, and beaten. Each glance at my own reflection was alarming. But I wasn't done and I decided to take my life back. I lost the weight, got back into shape, and made a conscious decision to prioritize my own health and well-being.

Now, I sing with a rock band and a country band, have appeared in the news for having had the nerve to promote my little business at a conference for entrepreneurial women, and frankly, I feel great. I wake up every morning looking forward to getting things done and moving forward. I'm meeting more people in real life who provoke me, inspire me, and engage with me professionally. It's a very exciting (although admittedly stressful) time.

Is my life perfect? Hell no. Do I look like a model? Ha ha ha. No. But I am *not* old. I am experienced. I am healthy. I am mostly happy. An involved and productive member of my community, I will very likely live a long time. And I will do everything in my power to keep from getting old. Because "old" is not an "age," but a state of mind. I will certainly age for the rest of my life, but I refuse to get old. I've been there, and it's not for me.

CHAPTER 47:
THE WARRIOR

August 8, 2012

Yoga helps keep me flexible and "sane." I attend a Monday night class regularly. At this point in my life, I am able to practice at home on my own, but the energy generated by a roomful of "yoginis" is pretty amazing. If you've never tried it, I highly recommend it.

One type of pose is called "The Warrior." There are several different "warriors," but they are all strong standing postures that project an assertive attitude. Assertion is what it's all about for me these days, and while I'm no shrinking violet, there are times when I need to steel myself to face the bureaucracies that enable me to cope financially with the cost of my mother's care. Warrior energy helps get me through it.

In Chapter 45, I spoke at length about my travails with my mother's long-term care insurance carrier. I had gotten so wrung out by the process, I finally wrote to their acting CFO to describe my ordeal and ask if revelation of my situation to the media was something they could afford. I received a phone call in response to that letter.

Turns out, they *have* been paying attention, and on further review, they owe me *more* money than I thought. The bills they had been reviewing from last summer were being reconsidered because they realized they'd made a mistake in calculating my mother's "elimination period." In the case of my mother's policy, this refers to the one hundred-day interval following the initial claim during which the insured is expected to self-pay their care. Once a claim is deemed valid, one hundred days after the claim is opened, the claimant qualifies for care in a facility. Before one hundred days, they would only pay for in-home care.[30] That was the route I had pursued for Mom, initially hiring caregivers to help in my home as my ability to deal with her condition became untenable.

Mom's journey was complicated exponentially by her contraction of a UTI, which landed her in five facilities over the course of three months.

I had long ago given up on ever being reimbursed for certain care my mother had received last year. But apparently the LTC carrier had not, and they were apologizing, revisiting, and promising to repay me for more of these expenses. I just had to resubmit one bill from the rehab facility Mom had been in (and ejected from for violent behavior) last June.

The representative who called me was sympathetic, kind, and finally, imparting good news. And this was apparently due, at least in part, to my taking the initiative, being assertive, and taking my case to another, higher level. I do appreciate the insurance company's willingness to hear my story and take corrective measures. I must give credit where it is due.

The moral of this story: when you feel beaten, don't surrender. Breathe, regroup, and take it to a higher level. You'll feel better. And you may even be heard. Because an assertive warrior is impossible to knock down and very hard to resist.

---

[30] Every policy is different, and the in-home care provision was more generous than many other policies. Always ask to have your benefits analyzed and explained by a professional.

CHAPTER 48:
ROCK STAR

September 25, 2012

"Tracey, can you please talk to your mom?"

Oh God, what now? Mom had called an hour ago. She was irrational and angry. She had hung up on me in disgust, unable to express the cause of her distress. I'd hoped I'd be able to get to my Monday night yoga class as planned.

"She got outside. She's trying to get out the fence. She's yelling 'Help!' at people on the street. She's got the phone and she won't give it back. She's picking up rocks and throwing them at me!"

Earlier, Karina[31] had attempted to give Mom a tranquilizer, but Mom threw the offered juice in her face. I don't know how she managed to get out the front door, but she'd clearly been agitated for a while.

From the number on my caller ID, I could see that this latest call was from Karina's own phone (since my mother had taken possession of the house phone).

"Can you turn on the speakerphone so she can hear me?"

"Yes." I could now hear the commotion from both sides. Mom was shrieking wildly for help from the cars passing her home.

"Mom. *Can you hear me?*"

---

[31] Not her real name.

"They're trying to kill me!"

"Mom? *Please. Put. The rocks. Down. Please, Mom. Please put them down.*" I kept my voice calm but firm.

She heard me. She put the rocks down. She went back into the house. She held onto the house phone.

Dressed in my yoga clothes, I had been preparing to go to my class, but Bob and I went to Ramsey instead. I was warned that 911 might be called and I didn't want to have to deal with police or emergency rooms. Bob was afraid Mom might try throwing rocks (or worse) at me, so he went along.

When we arrived, Mom was seated in the main dining area, calm as could be. The house phone had been liberated from her clutches. She was glad to see us, if a little sheepish. She realized she'd been overreacting to something and that her temper needed to be managed.

"I guess I have my father's temper." She had told me about my grandfather's dark side (although I'd never seen it).

"Sometimes I think you're channeling Herby," referring to my late father, whose temper was legendary.

"I keep losing him, that rat." Well, he's only been dead for eight years now.

"You see him here?"

"Yeah, he comes for a while and then he just disappears. There's never any intimacy. What's his name again?"

"Herby?"

Mom grinned and shook her head at herself. Not only did she keep losing him, now she was losing her ability to recall his name.

"It's okay, Mom."

She was getting tired. It was after 8 p.m. and she'd worn herself out. Karina caught my eye and lifted Mom's evening pill cup toward me to see if I'd dispense her meds. I nodded. She poured some juice as well and I took both cups to Mom.

She took them easily, throwing back the pills and drinking down the juice.

As we were getting ready to leave, Karina confided that as Mom was throwing the rocks at her, she'd commanded Karina to "Dance!" We all had to laugh at this.

Our job was done for the evening. Mom, the staff, and the phone were all safe inside. The rocks were safe outside. And Bob and I returned to our home, where I did a much-needed solo yoga practice and wound down for the evening.

That was one rock show I could have done without. Thankfully, the set was short and sweet.

CHAPTER 49:
SUPER MODEL

September 27, 2012

Due for another appointment with the retina specialist, I went to Ramsey to pick Mom up and bring her to the doctor's office in Wayne. Up in Mom's room, Sugar[32] was helping her get dressed. Of all the gals who take care of my mother, this lady is my favorite. Her sweet and caring nature radiate from her. Mom responds to her well. We agreed on a jacket for Mom to wear and made our way down the stairs.

A new resident, Simon,[33] stared at us as we got to the bottom of the stairs.

"This is my daughter," Mom told him proudly.

"Who?"

"This is my daughter," she told him again. Turning to me, she offered, "He's a little confused, like me. We're getting married."

"You're getting married and you didn't invite me?"

We all giggled at Mom's proclamation and I told Simon it was nice to meet him. We went out the door to the car down the driveway. I was glad to observe Mom's steady gait. Physical therapy did wonders.

---

[32] Not her real name.
[33] Not his real name.

During our travels to the eye doctor, Mom told me she had found Simon at another place and rescued him. She didn't love him, but she felt sorry for him and would marry him.

She also told me she had been to Paris last week. My brother screwed up the arrangements, so she got to the airport in Paris and then had to turn around and come back.

Mom also told me she'd won a beauty contest.

Back on Planet Earth, we went through the tests at the retina specialist's office. Mom reported worse vision and tooth problems to the eye technician. But the tests revealed that her vision was stable. Her good eye is still seeing at 20/30. The jury's out on her teeth (which are on an upper denture plate anyway).

Since we were in Wayne, near many retail stores, I took her to a shoe store and she tried on dozens. Finally, I found a glittery pair of black flats that fit her, which she could wear on Thanksgiving.

Did I know Mom had won a beauty contest?

I was grateful that Mom was so calm and pleasant. As we rode, I glanced at her on this bright, sunny, early fall day, and saw her smiling. She reached over and patted my hand. She was glad to be with me. Glad to feel cared for. Happy to be out and about with someone who loves and listens to her.

From rock star to supermodel, jetting to Paris and back, winning beauty contests and consenting to give her hand in marriage to a man she rescued, this was just another week in the life of my mother.

CHAPTER 50:
SUGAR PUSS

October 21, 2012

My caregiving life involves more than my mother. I also have my handsome tuxedo cat named Max who developed diabetes last year. He had a voracious appetite, but couldn't derive enough nutrition from his food as his pancreas was not making enough insulin to break down the nutrients to nourish him. Undigested sugar was "spilling" into his bloodstream and urine. He was perpetually thirsty, constantly urinating, and literally withering away.

Last November, Max's diabetes was diagnosed and a long process of adjusting his twice daily dosage of insulin began. We were initially horrified at the prospect of having to inject our boy every twelve hours, but as previously noted, he barely acknowledges the transaction (and often purrs loudly while it's happening).

Once the correct dosage was established, Max gained weight quickly and his clinical signs all became more normal. The dosage did have to be adjusted periodically, and I took him to the vet regularly to measure his blood glucose levels. In time, we got him down to 147. For cats and humans, 100 is considered good, but anything under 200 is acceptable. As we soon learned, a little high is way better than too low when it comes to blood glucose.

Part of our daily routine includes making fun of our cat. Max meows a lot. When he's hungry, thirsty, wanting attention or snacks, he's quite vocal. I do impressions of him, using a small squeaky voice to simulate his, providing snarky, silly commentary on how he must be feeling.

"Oh God, Mom, you have no idea what I've been through. My life sucks. Feed me, you negligent bitch!"

What's really funny is, more often than not, there's plenty of food left in his bowls when he's screaming for more; he's just forgotten it's there. He tries to get me to come to the utility room with him to ensure he'll be fed should the bowls be empty. And he's finicky; what he loves at one meal may not suit him at the next. There are even physical orientation issues I've discovered and documented.

As the morning progresses, I usually check on him to make sure he's not having a bad reaction. Late Friday morning, he seemed a little out of it. I tried to get him interested in a toy, but he wasn't going for it. Normally, he's pretty alert in the late morning and early afternoon, so I was concerned.

Max's vet had told me that if he seems lethargic, his blood sugar could be too low and could be addressed by rubbing syrup on his gums. I put a little maple syrup on my finger and applied it to his gums. His eyes widened immediately (I thought of the scene in the movie *Pulp Fiction* where John Travolta's character injects adrenaline into the chest of Uma Thurman's character) and Max bit my arm. It took a few minutes for me to realize I was bleeding, but I knew he wasn't being vicious; this was a reaction to the sudden spike in blood sugar. He clearly felt better, though, and I decided not to give him any insulin that night.

Saturday morning, I got up to feed Max at his regular time (7:30) and he met me at the door of the ground floor.

He meowed, but not frantically. (Some mornings, he comes up to the bedroom to get me moving, signaling greater urgency.) "About time you got down here" but not quite "Oh God! I'm starving!" I dished out some wet food and refreshed his crunchies. I also decided to decrease his insulin by one unit. I fed him, shot him, did some laundry, interacted with him a bit, and went back upstairs.

Bob called to me about an hour later. Bob had found Max hiding inside the living room sofa, something he hadn't done in a long time. He was howling, panting, drooling, and breathing heavily. I called the vet, described his symptoms, and told them we were bringing Max in.

Max is Bob's baby. He is absolutely crazy about this cat and tends to freak out in emergencies. He drove like a maniac and cursed every car impeding our progress on the scant mile to the vet's office. The second he'd parked, Bob grabbed the cat in the carrier from my lap and bolted through the door, parting the sea of people in the waiting room (Bob is 6 feet 7 inches, so people can't help but notice him), yelling, "Emergency! Out of the way!" I moved as quickly as I could to keep up.

Two new vets saw Max immediately, asked us some questions and they drew blood for a glucose test. The meter read "LO." That was bad. Max was going into hypoglycemic seizure. They shaved his forearm and started a catheter to deliver glucose and hydration to his bloodstream. He stopped screaming. The drooling ceased. The panting subsided. We wiped the slobber from his face and neck. Max got all bright-eyed as he watched the birds and squirrels scurrying around the birdfeeder outside the office window.

The doctors were kind and attentive. They suggested we leave Max for a couple of hours. They close early on Saturdays, and we might have to bring him to an emergency hospital for observation, but for now he was out of the woods.

Bob had gone out to the car to compose himself. He felt bad about bulldozing through all the other people in the waiting room and didn't want to be seen weeping. But there aren't many pet owners who couldn't relate to what they'd just witnessed. We all love our pets and will fight to get them relief from their distress. A lovely woman came over to talk to me, holding her kitty in her arms, as I sat in the waiting room, waiting for Max to be stabilized. She feared her cat was becoming diabetic. We traded stories of adopting and losing cherished pets. We've all been there. It's nice to talk to someone who understands.

We did go home for a bit. I managed to work out and shower. Bob had a little lunch and cleaned up. Then we went back to retrieve our boy.

Max was in a cage, the IV still attached. He meowed at us in acknowledgment on arrival.

"Oh God, you just don't know what I've been through! Get me out of here!"

Opening the cage door, he clearly wanted to leap out, but I wouldn't let him. I petted and comforted him. He leaned into me and I hugged him.

The doctor told me he thought Max was well enough to go home. No more insulin for the weekend. Let's try some diabetic food. Bring him in Monday for another blood glucose test and we'll see. He gave me his cell number so I could call him if anything happened over the weekend. Maybe the diabetes is in remission. It happens. Or maybe he just needs a lot less insulin. The titration process begins anew.

I just bought a brand-new vial of insulin, so it would be consistent with the pattern of my life that he wouldn't need it. And of course, it can't be returned. But if it turns out that Max doesn't need insulin ever again, I'll be happy to absorb that expense.

So, our little Sugar Puss is home, curled up in our bed and enjoying a quiet autumn weekend. Life is sweet for now.

CHAPTER 51:
SHEDDING LIGHT

January 25, 2013

"Sylvia" (me) and Mom

"Can you believe she's my sister?"

Gabriela[34] smiled patiently as she looked at me and tried to answer Mom's query.

"Well, it's probably a little easier for her to believe I'm your daughter, Ma."

---

[34] Not her real name.

My mother tends to think of me as her sister, Sylvia, these days. She also has this idea that Sylvia recently had twin babies. The actual Sylvia died in 2003 from pancreatic cancer. I am now fifty-five years old. Neither of us had twins. I don't know where Mom gets these ideas, but her creativity is fascinating.

We were chatting in Mom's new ground-floor room. I had requested this move after Mom fell down the stairs last July. She was now moved in, but the room upstairs had shelving where her many framed pictures could be easily placed around the perimeter. Down here, the pictures had to be hung with nails. I had contacted Connor,[35] one of the coordinators, about handling this. Today, my mission is to hang the pictures on the walls to make Mom's new space more homey.

"Would you like some tea or something hot to drink?" Mom offered. I didn't, but Mom did, so we went out to the kitchen and I got Mom's request in motion. As we sat and watched the president's inaugural festivities on TV, Connor arrived. I fixed Mom's tea, got her situated and told Connor I was ready when he was.

I laid the pictures out on Mom's bed and started placing them on the walls. Some of them only had easel backs and no hangers, so I placed those on flat surfaces.

Connor would climb up on his little ladder, tap in the nails and hang each framed photo in turn. He asked me about my mother's illness and how she came to live there.

I gave him the broad strokes and explained why I thought she was in the right place. He agreed. He'd been around and he said that it wasn't just because he worked there.

---

[35] Not his real name.

I asked him if he'd always wanted to work with older people. He said he just liked to help people, and that his brother was also a nurse who'd gotten into elder care before him.

It seemed like a good time to mention my new career in elder care. Having so much experience with my parents' needs, I recently decided to make a business of helping families cope with their elder care planning requirements. My new company, Light of Gray,[36] would provide guidance, resources and referrals.

Connor admitted that he had never looked at it from the family's perspective, that he had always approached it as a professional. I suggested that he might consider looking at his family's situation sooner than later.

It's funny, I expected that he might have a better handle on the issues than someone outside the business, but the truth is, if you have to do something for a living, you're inclined to separate yourself from the emotional components of the process so you can be more effective at your job. But it's not a good idea to let denial dictate your response to your own family's situation. Everyone needs help with some aspect of the process somewhere along the line.

I told him if he ever decided he needed help, I'd be delighted.

Mom came back in. How did she like it?

She pointed to the wedding picture of my brother and his wife over her bed. "I like that." She looked around the room and took it in. "So, you off now? What are you making for dinner?"

"I had been thinking about making a pot roast…"

---

[36] "Light of Gray" has since evolved into Grand Family Planning LLC.

"It's a little late for that now, isn't it?" at 4 o'clock. Yeah, Ma, you got me there.

She went back out to the living room and sat and chatted with one of her buddies. I had spotted Mom's glasses in her room and grabbed them for her, gently placing them on her face.

"Ah! That's better!" No wonder she didn't react to the pictures; she couldn't see them well.

I kissed Mom goodbye and waved to the others. Mission accomplished. I could return home to attend to making dinner and working on my business plan. Every day brings more opportunities, more ideas and the certainty that I'm on to something valuable.

CHAPTER 52:
SEEING THROUGH THE ANGER

February 17, 2013

Visiting my mother is not easy. I have to do it. I need to monitor what goes on at her group home and make sure she's getting everything she needs. Vigilance is required, because things change: Mom's condition, the staff, policies, and resident population mix at the home. So many variables can have an impact on Mom's quality of life.

Like any child, I've had my share of squabbles with my mother over the course of my life. That's only natural. But now, I never know who I'll find when I go to see her. The progress of her illness is unpredictable.

When I arrived at the home, I had trouble getting the bell to ring so I could be admitted. I called on my cellphone and was quickly greeted. I investigated the operation of the bell with Collin,[37] and then went in to see Mom.

She was seated in the main living area, watching TV. She rose to greet me, but was unsteady on her feet. I embraced her to help steady her. She complained that my hands felt cold to her (they always do) and I invited her to sit back down.

---

[37] Not his real name.

Recently, I'd had reports that Mom was behaving more aggressively and I'd asked to have urine cultures taken in case another UTI was brewing. Collin told me they had realized that one of the other residents was triggering Mom's behaviors. They used to sit together at meals; now they were being kept apart and Mom was doing better.

A new "activities director," Margaret,[38] had begun working there recently. She had given Mom a birthday party in January. Then she'd organized a Valentine's Day party. Margaret came over to show me pictures of the parties on the home's digital camera. We looked through the images together, seated at a table, with Mom sitting on my other side.

When I looked up from the camera, Mom had a puss on. Her lip was curled and she was angry. She told Margaret to pack up and get out. I asked Mom why she was upset.

Mom went on a tear about how she had never had sex with anyone but her husband and Mom seemed certain that Margaret was accusing her of wanton behavior. I had a hard time deciphering Mom's story, but her distaste for Margaret was unmistakable. I felt like maybe my paying too much attention to Margaret and the photos and not enough to her may have set her off.

For the rest of our visit, Mom's displeasure with her situation was clear. She hates everyone. She knows she's getting worse, but she can't help herself. She's angry. She's confused. She doesn't understand why her brother Bernie never calls. I reminded her that her brother had died a few years ago, making phone calls challenging.

She's the last of her tribe, the youngest of four children. And she was never very social when she was well. So it's just

---

[38] Not her real name.

her kids and grandkids remaining. Of the remainder, I'm the most involved. I'm her daughter, her sister, her mother, and therapist.

I observed and spoke with some of the other residents. Some of them are quite lucid, but they can't express themselves well. I overheard the resident with whom Mom allegedly clashes tell Margaret she just felt lost. My heart sank hearing her words. I felt for her, and my Mom, and all the others. That's really the crux of the matter. They're all "lost."

Trapped in a living body with a deteriorating mind. I can't imagine anything worse. I've no doubt that if I were in that position, I'd be pretty pissed off too.

For now, I'm a little sad. I'm glad I went. I know Mom's in good hands, getting appropriate care. That's the best I can do for her. And I will continue this process as long as she needs me to.

And I will do everything I can to escape a similar fate.

CHAPTER 53:
A QUICKIE

July 1, 2013

At a recent "Longest Day" event held at her group home (an Alzheimer's fundraising and awareness-raising event held on June 20 each year), one of the nurses who used to work with Mom came for a visit. She told Mom how nice she looked. Mom said, "You can thank my embalmer."

CHAPTER 54:
AT THE HOLIDAYS

December 9, 2013

It's been some time since my last post and I suspect it will be a while before I post again. I wanted to give folks a little update. Mom is still with us, although her language capabilities continue to deteriorate. She is becoming more incontinent and her time in our shared reality continues to diminish.

I spent time with her at a luncheon at her group home the day before Thanksgiving. She had just had an "accident." She was more confused than usual and glassy-eyed. I asked the nurse manager if she had a fever. She didn't. Her appetite, which is usually excellent, was poor. I asked for a urine culture to be taken.

Mom was able to join the rest of the family at my brother's house on Thanksgiving Day. She was very confused, but her appetite was good and she recognized her grandchildren as family. I noted further UTI symptoms.

My suspicions regarding her infection were confirmed and Mom is being treated.

The moral of this story is no matter where you decide to place your loved one, make sure you can get there to visit on regular basis. Be observant, partner with the staff, and say what's on your mind. Hug your loved one; they'll feel better, even if they can't remember why. The emotional part of their brain continues to function long after the reasoning and memory areas are gone.

Have a wonderful holiday season and feel good about the difference you make in the lives of the people who need you most.

CHAPTER 55:
HAPPY NEW FEARS

December 29, 2013

My husband is in a quandary about how to spend New Year's Eve. He remarked this week about how his favorite celebration in the last few years was the one we spent at home, toasting the arrival of the New Year with champagne in our hot tub. That year (2010) had been especially trying as Mom's condition had taken a severe turn for the worse. I had wished for the strength to cope with what was to come and got my wish.

This year has been challenging too, and I suppose each year in one's life must be. Bob lost his job of eleven years in September 2012 and started a new one in February 2013. He hated it so much, it made his blood pressure escalate to the point of requiring medication. I encouraged him to quit after six months. He did, and started a new job in September. This job is better and pays considerably more, and I'm grateful. The hours are long, but he likes the work and his colleagues. So he's poised for a happier new year.

I started a new career path in March as a natural extension of my elder care exploits. I was recruited by a major financial services company and graduated to becoming a financial advisor in August. It's a great company and I love the potential of what I can do to help people. But it's hard! Persuading people to sit down and talk to me about grown-up stuff is not easy. My passion to get families talking and considering their futures does come through and I am determined to make headway in this profession in 2014.

Mom is appreciably worse. I'm glad she's acclimating to her home. But her language capabilities are suffering and her physical coordination is failing. And her long-term care funds are down to about another year where she is. I'm going to have to make some decisions.

No one knows how long a person may live. Mom can go on like this for years to come. I have resources to keep her where she is for a while. But on a long enough time line, the ugly specter of Medicaid will have to be considered. And I really hate that idea.

Clearly, she can't live with us. Been there, done that. It's too dangerous for all of us. But if the money I put aside starts running out, I'll need a "Plan B," which may have to involve "Plan M" (as in Medicaid).

More grown-up stuff to contemplate. Doesn't it ever get easier? Some days, yes. Others, no.

If you find yourself in need of talking to someone about planning for your family's future, I highly recommend working with a professional. I always have, even before becoming one. Working with the right people can save you money, aggravation, and heartache.

Wishing you and yours a happy, healthy, and peaceful New Year. And don't feel pressured to go out to celebrate. Sometimes the best times are the simplest, if you're lucky. I know I am. Cheers!

CHAPTER 56:
HE'S LICKING MY TOES!

March 8, 2014

As I headed to my office, I went through my mental checklists. I was grateful that the weather was clear, even if it was frigid. I would go home around noon, and pick up Mom's fur for her to wear so she would be comfy as we drove to the retina specialist this afternoon.

My phone rang; it was June,[39] the head nurse at Mom's home. Mom had fallen and bumped her head. She didn't seem badly injured, but she said her head hurt.

"Please send her to the ER. I'll meet her there."

I went to my office, rescheduled my morning phone conference, touched base with colleagues, canceled Mom's appointment with the retina doctor, and headed to the hospital.

Mom was there, having her blood drawn. I asked the nurse if a urinalysis was done.

It was on the list. Could Mom use a bedpan?

Good question. Her capabilities have been on the decline, but I thought we should try. A catheter isn't fun.

---

[39] Not her real name.

The nurse helped Mom roll onto a bed pan. I talked to her and tried to get her to pee. She amiably jabbered to me. She was glad to see her big sister (she often confuses me, her child, with her older sister, who passed in 2003).

After a time, we asked Mom if she was able to pee.

"My husband is frannish."

I looked at the nurse and said, "Hey, I was wondering, do you think maybe she has dementia?"

She laughed and rolled Mom off the pan. No pee. A straight catheter would be employed.

The procedure was professionally administered but tough to witness.

The tests were all done pretty quickly; CAT scan, EKG, blood, urine. Then we waited. And waited.

Mom got antsy. She kicked off her blankets and wanted to get up. Her eyes were glassy. She pointed to people and critters I could not see.

I got hungry, made sure the nurses knew I was stepping away, and made my way to the café. I bought two cups of chicken soup and a panini. I went back to Mom's room and found a table so she could eat the soup without wearing too much of it. She ate well.

Finally, after about four hours, the doctor on call came in. Mom had another UTI. Nothing broken, no other concerns. So she would get Bactrim and a ride home.

I thought about taking her home myself, but aside from the fact that she had no coat, she was not mobile. She couldn't go to the bathroom without two strong helpers. She was like a 170-pound infant.

Once I got transportation arranged, Mom sat in a wheelchair, donning hospital gown, diaper, and hospital socks (she had peed on her own socks and I gave the nurse permission to toss the soiled ones). I kissed her goodbye, and she giggled, pointing to her feet. "Look, he's licking my toes!"

I'm so glad her hallucinations are happy ones!

I went to Mom's home, dropped off the prescription and release orders with June, and comforted Mom's girlfriend. Jenny[40] loves my Mom and always hugs me when I visit. She seems so lucid, until you chat for more than a few minutes. I reassured her that Mom was fine and coming back. For now.

My concern is that with Mom's history, it doesn't take a rocket scientist to figure out when she's having a UTI, and I may have to move her to a place that's more observant and proactive. I have a friend who's a geriatric care manager (remember "Julia Roberts?"), who knows and loves my mother, and has other places I can consider. Next week, we resume exploring options.

Meanwhile, I've made sure Mom will get her meds and physical therapy. Her active imagination should take care of the rest.

---

[40] Not her real name.

CHAPTER 57:
ANOTHER MOVING EXPERIENCE

June 8, 2014

Settling in at her new place

For the last three years, my mom has lived in two memory care group homes. When she arrived in her first one, she was at an awkward stage of her illness; she had moderate dementia and profound psychosis. She'd been in and out of a psychiatric hospital due to violent behavior and attempts to escape captivity.

Finding a place that would accept her and cope with her behaviors was a challenge. A small group home was a good solution.

Mom's behaviors were triggered by groups of people talking in front of her and not including her. Paranoia would compel her to think she was being "set up." She'd try to defend herself with butter knives. Or rocks. Or bags of chips. Whatever was handy. So her placement in a group home with half a dozen residents (and three caregivers) was a good way to minimize her triggers. But at the same time, she was still a lot more lucid than most of the other residents, and she was miserable. I cried a lot after those visits and had to work through it to be able to accept that of all possible solutions, this was the best I could do for her.

In time, Mom adjusted, and even enjoyed a little romance. When the freak Halloween snowstorm of 2011 hit, Mom's home in Montville lost power and she was moved to Ramsey. It was a good move. There were mostly women residents at the new place. One resident who had clashed with Mom was moved to another home, and she found some buddies at the new place. And Ramsey is a lot more geographically convenient for me.

I have been pretty satisfied with the care Mom's received, but we are now in the last year of her four-year, long-term care insurance policy. The rent has gone up from 4,990 dollars/month to 5,450 dollars. Another bump could be expected in July. And they are starting to charge an additional 250 dollars per quarter for "Medicare assessments."

Having established a working relationship with a geriatric care manager ("Julia Roberts," who helped place Mom in the first group home), I was offered a deal for Mom at a new place. This facility is the same type of home, but with more residents (the capacity is forty, but there are presently more like twenty). Recently converted from a psychiatric facility, they are seeking more residents. It's run by a nice, caring family and it's located in Montclair. The rent is two thousand dollars less than the place where Mom's been living. And that's before the anticipated 2014 increase.

After checking on the nearby hospital and servicing medical personnel, I submitted the facility to review by Mom's long-term care insurance provider. They gave it the thumbs up.

The only downside is the travel time; it's forty minutes from my home. But it's only about twenty minutes from my office, so it's really not that bad.

I moved Mom last week. Prepared for the worst, I took time off from work to move her and support her through the transition as necessary.

On moving day, I cleaned out Mom's old room. The only furniture she has now is a bookcase. She has a lot of clothing, pictures, and tchotchkes. She also has a big, fat, red Chinese Buddha and a Sandicast dog (that looks eerily real). Bob and I packed the stuff in two cars. When it was time to leave, Mom didn't want to go. There was a woman playing piano and singing songs with the residents. I don't think her reluctance to leave was attachment to the home so much as not wanting to leave the entertainment.

I drove Mom to the new place. She was pretty quiet. I tried to converse with her, but her language skills have deteriorated. I played music and sang to her. She smiled.

When we got to the new place, residents were sitting outside, enjoying the air. Many of them are cigarette smokers. They greeted all of us warmly.

The staff members came out and hustled Mom's stuff out of the cars and into the home. They told me not to worry. They would wash Mom's clothes, unpack, and set up her room.

Really? I could just go?

Yes; in fact, it was better if we went. Give her a couple of days to settle in.

After reviewing the paperwork and writing some checks, I was done.

Wow. "Just go." I kissed Mom goodbye, and off I went.

Days went by. I texted my friends at the new home. How was Mom doing?

Fine. Eating well. No fights. Conversing pleasantly.

Yesterday, I got a call. Mom fell. She wasn't hurt. She bruised her hip, but she was fine.

Today, a week later, I decided to pop in. I was greeted warmly by the residents on the porch. I entered and Mom was sitting in her chair.

"Tracey!" My mother recognized me and called me by my name. Over the last six months, she had usually referred to me as her big sister, Sylvia. On one recent visit, she looked at me blankly and hardly reacted at all.

But today, I was Tracey, her daughter. She was very glad to see me. No complaints. No aches or pains. She chattered and tried to converse. She has seen "Herby" (my father, who's been gone nearly ten years). She pointed out a big, heavyset fellow who was the apparent stand-in for her absent husband.

Lunch was served. It looked pretty good and smelled delicious. Mom ate well and had a couple of desserts and coffee too.

Mom's big red Buddha, "Mike," was in the dining room, blessing all who came to eat. I like that.

Inspecting her room, I appreciated the way they set it up. Pictures and albums nicely stored and arranged, clothing hung neatly in the closet or folded in drawers.

Her dog was in the living room. Quite the conversation piece, many of the residents wanted to feed her or give her water.

I did notice Mom's hands were shaky. I mentioned this to "Julia Roberts." She smiled and said, "Guess who just arrived?" Mom's new doctor.

I had a very good relationship with Mom's previous geriatrician, so I was a little reticent about the change. But I was glad I was there to meet her new primary care provider. He had a very reassuring manner and great, firm handshake. I gave him Mom's history and he was appreciative. I felt very blessed with the timing. I like to know who my partners in care are.

My next appointment was pending and I had to get going, but as I kissed Mom goodbye and headed out, I felt really good about this transition. Sometimes, when you work at it, the stars begin to align and the universe brings you what you need.

Today, I am grateful and hopeful that what remains of my mother's life will be as pleasant, comfortable and enjoyable as possible. Life is short. Except, of course, when it isn't.

And so I am moved to say a few things:

1. I am profoundly grateful to be able to take care of my mother without killing myself.
2. Know that this was possible because my family *planned*. We could not envision this, but the likelihood that my parents would need some care at the end of their lives was high.
3. It still sucks to go through. It is painful to watch someone you love deteriorate.
4. It's easier to endure when you have a team behind you to help you cope. I am blessed to have a great team.

CHAPTER 58:
THE GRAY LINE

July 4, 2014

During a more wakeful moment at rehab

Mom seemed to be settling nicely into her new home. I was glad she found a boyfriend (and as per her recent pattern, soon dumped him for another one). Then her falls started.

The first one yielded a bruised hip. X-rays at the local hospital revealed no fracture. A week later, Mom had a scuffle with a caregiver and fell. She complained of soreness, so she was sent to the hospital again. This time, her blood work showed a very high white count. She had moved from the familiar realm of urinary tract infections to a new, far more dangerous one: sepsis.

Mom had an infection in her bloodstream. This apparently evolved from an unchecked UTI. She needed IV antibiotics. Unfortunately, in her condition, she tends to pull out her IVs, leaving nasty tears in her skin. She had to be restrained.

The infection was identified and could be treated with oral antibiotics, so she could be freed from IVs and restraints.

During this hospitalization, I thought Mom was going to die. She looked terrible. She was mostly unconscious. Her first day, she ate with assistance, with her eyes closed the whole time.

The next day, after a course of IV antibiotics, I found her sitting up in a recliner, alert and watching TV. She chatted with me a bit. She was off her psych meds and was a little clearer than usual. Next visit, she was passed out again.

After about a week, the infection was under control, and Mom's doctor felt she could be transferred to a rehabilitation facility for reconditioning. I worked with the social workers at the hospital to find a suitable place.

Mom was transferred, but she needed clothes. All she had were the clothes on her back from when she had been admitted to the hospital, where supplied gowns were all she needed. In rehab, she would need clothing.

The facility called my brother first (I suspect his mother-in-law had been in the same facility at some point and his number was on file) and the caller told him about Mom's need for clothes. He told them to reach out to me for decisions, but he texted me to ask if I wanted him to handle the clothing request. I gratefully accepted the offer. He bought her new blouses, sweatpants, socks, and a bra and sent them by UPS overnight. She would have them Thursday morning.

Meanwhile, that Wednesday, the facility called me about paperwork, and I went down, bringing sneakers for Mom. I filled out the paperwork and went upstairs to see her.

She was sitting in a wheelchair in the day room. She was on oxygen. She didn't seem to know me. She was pretty out of it. I didn't stay long.

I returned that Saturday with Bob. Once again, she was in the day room wearing the same clothes she had been wearing the previous Wednesday. She was still in a fog, but she did interact with us. I asked about the clothing my brother had sent. No one knew anything.

I spent a good deal of time trying to track down my mother's lost items, but on a weekend, it was an uphill battle. I went to Mom's home and picked up some things from her room and ran them back to the rehab. I inventoried the items with the staff and went back to check on Mom, who was still in the day room. Did she remember that we had just been there? Do you remember seeing Bobby?

"Yeah, he was sitting right next to me."

Okay, she registered something.

On Monday, I worked the phones until I got a hold of someone who could help and I got confirmation that her clothes were found and she would be wearing them.

Tuesday, I returned to find Mom slumped in her wheelchair, completely unresponsive. She would not open her eyes. She wouldn't react. I went to the nurses.

Mom's blood work was bad. They gave me all the specifics and told me what they intended to do. I called Mom's doctor. I was alarmed. Had she been released from the hospital too soon?

They told me it was my decision. Mom is DNR: Do Not Resuscitate. Do Not Intubate. Do Not Hospitalize. I could change my mind at any time, but sending her to the hospital would mean aggressive, life-extending treatment.

Wow. This was a first. This was not black or white. I had hit a gray line. I was prepared to let Mom die if it was clearly her time. But here I was, unsure. Was she getting appropriate treatment? Or was she being mistreated in some significant way that was accelerating her decline? I was working with a new team and I sincerely didn't know what to do.

I called her doctor's office again. I was told he would call me back, but he didn't. So I called his office in the morning and got his recorded message, which provided his cell number. I sent him a text asking him to please call me. And he did.

The doctor told me Mom had been put back on her psych meds and they were probably the cause of her extreme fatigue. He would take her off them.

When I visited later that day, a physical therapist was adjusting Mom's chair and chatting with her. Mom was alert. She didn't know me until I told her who I was and she smiled broadly and kissed me.

The therapist told me Mom was able to stand up and they had played balloon volleyball. They demonstrated. She remarked that Mom's range of motion in her arms was good. She also observed that Mom had a good sense of humor.

Clearly, Mom was a whole lot better.

Today, I met with Mom's team to discuss her plan of care and to review what the goals were. We're trying to get her mobile enough to go back to the home, where she can walk with a walker, get around, and be a little more steady on her feet. I wasn't expecting miracles, just a little better quality of life.

Mom's speech therapist told me she enjoyed Mom's sense of humor. Showing Mom a pen, she had asked if Mom knew what the object was.

"A fountain pen."

Did she know what it was used for?

Mom made a remark that the therapist did not wish to repeat, but she blushingly indicated that Mom knew exactly what she was saying and let the therapist know that if she didn't know what to do with the pen, Mom was willing to show her where to put it.

So the line becomes a lighter gray for now, as we work to restore Mom to some kind of condition that allows her to resume the life she had before sepsis, with a little of the old, funny Mom sprinkled in for good measure.

CHAPTER 59:
PAPERED

July 20, 2014

Having gotten into a groove with Mom's care over the last few years, I've been spared from the kind of ongoing, overwhelming bureaucracy one encounters at the beginning of the caregiving journey. There are tasks to which I've had to attend regularly, but they've been manageable. Unfortunately, when major changes occur, an avalanche of paperwork ensues.

Moving Mom to a new facility took some doing. It meant exit communication for the old place (giving adequate notice to minimize the cost of leaving), entrance paperwork, establishing relationships with new staff, doctors, and providers, verifying insurance coverage, setting up evaluations, and ensuring everyone was doing their job. I do not like to micromanage, but sadly, oversight must be implemented if you want to get things done; the current business climate puts little emphasis on customer service or quality control, so trust no one.

Mom's care is complicated by the fact that she is highly vulnerable to infections and is also fairly inarticulate. UTIs (and recently, sepsis) have weakened her and have had a huge impact on her cognition, communication, and physical abilities. I have been trying to get her the personal care she needs as well as physical therapy. Rehab facilities only go so far. When a patient can't speak for themselves (as is the case with my mother), they tend to get lost in the shuffle. Consequently, I sought alternatives to facility-managed therapy.

And I have needed to involve Mom's health insurance company. I have her in managed Medicare, so there are a lot of compromises: the insurer covers much more than traditional Medicare, as long as the providers are in-network.

Add to that the requirements of my life: I have a full-time position with a financial services company, not to mention my husband, a cat with diabetes, clients from my graphic arts/video business, and a rock band. I have been trying to work while managing Mom's needs, but I finally decided to take Family Leave in order to be able to focus on Mom's care. I also needed to apply for Family Leave benefits with the state (my company does not pay for time off). So that means paperwork to my company's administration, Human Resources, and the state of New Jersey.

Is anyone else cognizant of the irony of having to take time off in order to apply for time off?

So here I am, organizing, making my lists, aggregating forms, trying to make sure I'm getting them filled out properly, and following up with Mom's doctors to make sure they fill out the medical certifications for all the parties involved. This is *not* easy; just getting a return phone call for a medical emergency is tough enough; responding to requests for administrative stuff for little old me? Oh, sure, right. Take a number.

I will say I am grateful to my employers for encouraging me to take the time and providing the administrative resources to document the need. But I will be happy when I can look back at this chapter in the printed ledger of my life with amusement and gratitude that I got through it with my wits and sense of humor intact. Until then, print, sign, fax, mail, call, shred, repeat.

CHAPTER 60:
HERB'S EYE VIEW

August 11, 2014

Working on a video project today, I was thinking about some family footage I hadn't viewed in a long time. I located the tape. This particular VHS cassette holds memories my father recorded between 1985 and 1997. There's more than two hours of material. Some of it, I'd never watched before.

Seeing my father in middle age, hearing his voice, listening to his jokes, witnessing his engagement with his family, often from behind the lens, brought such a mix of emotions. I felt comforted, happy, sad, frustrated, sometimes a little bored. I wanted to go back to some of the places he'd shot. I felt nostalgic for his company, for our shared past, particularly once we became friends. He was a great listener and gave wonderful advice.

Of course, I can't go back. The houses in the footage are now inhabited by other families. So much of my family is gone now. The places are empty without the people who mattered, the phantoms in the footage.

My father was not a religious man. His family wasn't, and when my parents lost their first son at eighteen months of age to meningitis, I think any faith he might have had before that terrible loss was extinguished. But I did find an interesting moment on the tape that provided a window into my father's later-life views.

The apartment my parents shared in southern Florida was on the fourteenth floor of their building. It faced southeast, and had an amazing view of the Atlantic Ocean and the Intracoastal Waterway. Early one Sunday morning, my father took his camcorder out on the terrace and shot the sun rising over the ocean. My father can be heard ruminating about what a beautiful day it would likely be, following a boat as it motored up the Intracoastal toward open water. Speaking softly, in his gruff but gentle manner, I heard him say, "Roz and I get up in the morning and we feel all right, and we hear that everything up north is okay, and we say, 'Thank you God.'"[41]

At the end of my father's life, his misery was so profound, all he wished for was death. He told me that every time he woke up, he was disappointed. His desire, expressed so clearly, made it a little easier for us to let him go. His passing ten years ago was truly a blessing. As I've said before, I really lost him about a year before he died.

Being able to connect today with his happier times is such a great gift. Knowing he had a long, happy interval, where he experienced joy, gratitude, and a connection to a higher power, whatever it might have been for him, makes me so grateful he captured it. And rediscovering it now is a wonderful reminder that life is meant to be enjoyed, savored, and appreciated while you can. Thank you, Herby. I'm so lucky to have known you, and I'm so glad you left a record of some of those good times.

---

[41] The clip may be viewed on YouTube: https://youtu.be/ u5vEE8Z_9E8

CHAPTER 61:
ROLLER COASTER

August 29, 2014

No matter how long I spend on the caregiver road, I am often surprised at how I can still be surprised.

Following a hospital stay for sepsis (and a purposely short stay in rehab), I got my mother back to the best possible care at her group home residence. I was not happy with the care she was receiving at the rehab. Back at the group home, she was bathed daily (compared to once every five days at the other facility). She wore her own clean clothes and received affectionate attention from caregivers and other residents. Augmented by in-home physical therapy to get her stronger, she was responding well. She was gaining strength, the ability to stand with help, and to walk with a walker. The aides at the home expressed their pleasure with her progress. That was Friday.

Saturday morning I got the call: she was back in the hospital. Mom was bleeding from her intestines.

On arrival at the ER, my brother was already there. The ER doctor told me Mom had lost a lot of blood and might need a transfusion. I told her Mom is DNR; there would be no transfusion. I was cautioned that Mom could have a heart attack or stroke. I let her know I understood. I turned to my brother.

"You understand where I'm going with this, right?"

He indicated he did, and agreed. She wouldn't want to extend her life. If she were a pet, I'd have taken her to the vet and ended it by now. And it would be the right thing. Unfortunately, it's not the *legal* thing.

Mom was admitted. Her nurse told me Mom's blood work was abnormal. Her hemoglobin was high, but that had to be a mistake. How could anyone lose so much blood and have a high red count?

Two young interns came in to examine Mom. I gave them her history and they looked her over. They were sweet and attentive. They gave me their phone numbers.

Over the course of her stay, I learned something that really rocked me: Mom's blood work was correct. Her red blood cell count *was* high. Apparently, she's had that rare condition, Polycythemia Vera, probably for years. Her bone marrow makes too many red blood cells, which can cause clots (like the one she reported feeling in her chest in 2006 when she had a heart attack). It's also associated with a lot of other symptoms, like dizziness, gout, bleeding ulcers (all of which she's had), aphasia (speech problems), confusion, and memory and perception issues. This could, indeed, be the true cause of her dementia, and may explain why her symptoms are so atypical of Alzheimer's.[42]

This condition apparently caused the intestinal bleeding too. It's her body's way of casting off all the extra hemoglobin clogging her circulatory system. Her red blood cell count went closer to normal levels as a result of her bleeding out. (In fact, treatment for this condition involves bloodletting.)

---

[42] She did, in fact, have Alzheimer's Disease as well as Polycythemia Vera. The Alzheimer's was confirmed by tests done as part of a study in which Mom participated, about a year after she died.

For a patient with the ability to cooperate and recuperate, the doctors would have performed an endoscopy. We all agreed that submitting Mom to that misery was pointless.

My geriatric care manager (aka Julia Roberts) told me that, based on her vast experience with the elderly, Mom was breaking down. This was probably a good time to consider hospice. Mom's doctor agreed.

I also wanted to get Mom out of the hospital. She was being left unattended for long stretches. She wasn't bathed. They kept her in the same gown, with pressure cuffs and foam booties on her legs and IVs in her arms (all of which she tried to remove). She was unable to press a button or call out for help. I had to go in every day to check and make sure she was getting fed and hygienically tended. Every time I saw her, she was cognitively worse, hallucinating and speaking in tongues.

A nurse actually asked me what language Mom spoke. I said, "Rozese." (Mom's nickname was "Roz" and this was her very own language.)

She was released the following Thursday, and I coordinated her hospice assessment with her arrival back at the residence. That evening, when I got there, Mom was in a new room. This double room could accommodate a hospital bed and put her closer to the hub of activities, so she could be attended to more readily. She was in bed and quite giddy. She laughed at jokes I told her. She clearly connected with her caregiver. (I had not met the night gal before.) This woman expressed obvious affection for my mother and it was definitely mutual.

The hospice nurse arrived to evaluate Mom and go through the paperwork with me. She was very kind and patient. When she asked me if I understood hospice, I told her what I knew: that the goal is to provide comfort and freedom from pain. No life-extending measures would be taken.

She was impressed and probably a little relieved. Most people in this situation haven't come around to certain realities. I was already there.

She also told me something very interesting: her father had died at forty-seven from the condition Mom has! He was born the same year as Mom. He died on the way to the hospital thirty-eight years ago. It's amazing how such a rare disease can suddenly seem like an epidemic.

Now that I have accepted this course, there are things I can and can't do for Mom. She can't receive physical therapy any longer; that's considered life-preserving. She can go to the hospital if she breaks a bone or something of that nature. She can come off hospice and go back on any time, as needed. I can always change my mind.

Will I? Who knows? How long will this go on? Can she possibly continue this way for months or years on end? Could life be that cruel?

It's beyond good days and bad days; it's good moments and bad moments. She's tired all the time. She knows me, then she doesn't. She chatters unintelligible gibberish, and then speaks a name or thought rather clearly. Up and down. High and low. Dead and alive. The roller coaster ride continues, and I long to get off.

I'm tired. I'm sad. I'd like to talk to someone, but I can't think of who right now.

So I write. I type out the toxins, the sadness, the pain, the knowledge, all of it. I pray for the end to her suffering. I pray for the end of the ride, so I can get on with my life. I don't expect miracles. But part of me continues to ask.

CHAPTER 62:
SO GIFTED

December 6, 2014

Growing up, I was often disappointed by my parents' lack of attention to my needs. We were not at all wealthy, and my folks had other things on their minds. The baby doll I had to have, the cool watch I really wanted for my birthday, a bike that could be adjusted for my short little legs – these material gifts occasionally appeared, but usually long after the initial urgency had abated.

What I appreciate most about my upbringing is that I learned to *value* things. My parents encouraged me to work for what I wanted. I did chores at home for my allowance. I got my working papers at fourteen and got a part-time job while still in high school. I haven't stopped working since.

I've always loved to give gifts. Knowing someone well enough to guess what might please them, presenting the carefully wrapped item, watching as the accompanying card is read, feeling the anticipation as the paper comes off and witnessing the response. Getting it right is so satisfying.

As my mother aged, she would try to give me her stuff. While I appreciated that she no longer needed certain things and wanted them to go to good use, it was hurtful to me when she'd try to return something I'd given her. Once her independent life ended, my perspective changed. I rescued a number of things she could no longer keep. I gave away much more than I kept.

Now, the kinds of gifts my mother gives me come through her windows of lucidity. These are double-edged swords that cut (at least) two ways.

This year, my mother's condition has deteriorated a great deal, and she hallucinates constantly. Her speech is incomprehensible most of the time. She mutters, talks to people I can't see, and she can't stand to wear her dentures, making her articulation worse. I typically spend about an hour with her at her group home, watching her rip up magazines, roll up paper tubes, reach for things only she can see, calling out to who knows whom. I hug her, kiss her, try to talk to her. I ask if she knows me, and she shrugs. Eye contact is rare.

As I get ready to leave, something clicks and she plugs in for a moment. And that's when she gives me the goods.

In August, after I'd seen her through her bought of sepsis, she gave me a big one. She'd slept on a sofa through most of my visit at the home while I hugged and sang to her. I was taking my leave, saying goodbye. Suddenly alert and seated in her wheelchair, she looked me straight in the eye, and clearly told me, "Don't feel guilty for leaving me here." (I didn't, but it was great to hear it from her.)

In November, as I kissed her goodbye, she looked at me and asked simply, "You know what I do?"

"No Ma, what?"

"Love you."

I made it home, told my husband what she had said, and cried.

Last week, after an hour of no conversation whatsoever, as I rose to leave and kissed her cheek, she said, "Be careful how you go. I love you."

My mother has a good appetite and eats well. She no longer receives any medications, as her prognosis is so poor. She's still on hospice, a service that provides comfort and monitors her for pain.

Her affection for her caregivers is evident. On some level, in the shifting quicksand of her existence, my mother knows she's in the right hands, that she is loved and she will never be alone or afraid. And that's one of the last gifts I'm able to give her.

Letting me know that she knows is one of the last gifts she's able to give me.

Enjoy your life, and please let those you love know how you feel. Shared presence is the best present of all.

CHAPTER 63:
END OF THE RIDE

April 18, 2015

My phone rang while I was exercising at home on the last day of March 2015. The hospice nurse attending to Mom called to suggest I get down there soon. "She's transitioning." This is hospice-speak for "her body is breaking down and she will die soon." Mom had not been eating, and she was having trouble breathing. She was given oxygen to make her more comfortable and was in bed, resting. She was in no immediate danger, but she was getting closer to the finish line after eight months in hospice limbo.

I texted my brother, who was in California on business. I urged him not to rush home. It was simply an update. I had a business appointment and kept it.

Upon arrival at Mom's group home, her caregivers told me Mom had become alert before the hospice nurse left, drank a big glass of orange juice and ate a big bowl of applesauce. Her hands had been turning blue, but the oxygen helped perk and pink her up. I went into her room. I tried to wake her, gently, but to no avail. She looked horrible. The resemblance between the body in the bed and the mother I had known was almost nonexistent.

I went home and thought, April is going to be the month.

The next morning I called the home to see how Mom was doing.

"Oh, she's fine! She's getting dressed and ready for breakfast. She's joking around. She's back to normal." This was no April Fool's joke, but it sure felt like one. Rallyin' Rozzy. The roller coaster ride continues, and it's making me nauseous.

I visited her the following week. Once again, she was in bed in the afternoon. No oxygen this time. She was just out of it. I looked under the sheets at her body. She had lost a great deal of weight. Her left leg was a stick. Her right leg looked more "normal." I rubbed her shoulders and arms. After a while, her eyes fluttered open and she looked at me. I said, "Hi," she said, "Hi" back; then she closed her eyes.

On the morning of Tuesday, April 14, I texted my brother and sister-in-law to wish them a happy anniversary, thirty-one years together. They had married on our parents' thirty-third anniversary.

I had a lunch appointment, and as we were winding up our meeting, my phone rang. Through the din at the restaurant, I heard the hospice nurse say Mom was "active" and didn't expect to see her again.

My first thought was, oh no, Mom's getting violent again. But "active" is hospice-speak for "actively transitioning to death." Mom's first big dose of morphine had been administered and she was not expected to live through the night.

All at once it struck me. It's April 14, her wedding anniversary. Herby is finally coming for her. She's going home.

I welled up and apologized to my colleague. Of course she understood and suggested I call my husband to drive me to see Mom. My first impulse is always, "Oh, I've got this. I'm fine." But then I thought, she's right. I called Bob and told him what was happening and that I needed him to drive. Of course, he understood.

Then I called my brother. Texting wasn't appropriate for this message. I wanted to make sure he fully grasped the situation. He did, and said he'd get there soon.

I drove home to meet Bob in Ringwood and we headed down to Montclair.

My brother's car was parked out front. The staff greeted me and told me my brother was with Mom, and that the hospice nurse had just left.

Standing by the bed, my brother gazed at the unconscious remains of our dying mother. Tears rolled down his face as he reported what the nurse had told him. In a whisper, he thanked me for taking care of all this.

We sat on the other bed in the room and started looking through Mom's photo albums. I could have taken them home long ago. She hadn't been able to look at them for months. But now they gave us a way to connect with the person Mom had been.

One album contained photos of my parents at the start of their "renaissance." In 1984, the year my brother married, Dad had undergone coronary bypass surgery. He was given a great second chance, and he took it. He had an epiphany while he was recovering from the procedure: he hadn't been the best husband up to that point, and he realized he loved his wife and wanted to make amends to her. So he went into semi-retirement, started taking trips with Mom and gearing up for a nice retirement. He bought a waterfront house at the Jersey Shore. He got into boating. They sold their house in Brooklyn and bought their apartment in Florida.

Their first holiday together in 1984 was a cruise. We had seen them off from the piers on the west side of New York City. At that time, Mom and Dad were in their fifties, the age we're at now. In the pictures, Mom looked stunning.

My brother snapped some of the images with his phone and posted them on Facebook. He was starting to have some epiphanies of his own.

The room was warm, and one of the residents kept popping in and saying distracting things, so we'd closed the door, making it stuffier. Mom occasionally made little groaning or gurgling sounds. She seemed peaceful, though, and her breathing was steady.

I'll admit this, because it may help others going through this process: "A watched Mom never dies." I know that sounds horrible, but I felt that she wasn't quite ready to go, and it wasn't essential for us to witness her final breath.

I suggested that we didn't have any obligation to stay; it was our choice. I further advised my brother to go to his wife and have a nice dinner together to celebrate their anniversary as best they could. I'd call him when I got the word. He nodded and we all left.

Bob and I headed back toward home. He suggested the fancy Italian place in our town, but I thought China Paradise, a classic Chinese restaurant in Wayne, was a better choice. Mom loved Chinese and she'd enjoyed that place with us.

We had a nice meal and toasted Mom. When the bill came with the fortune cookies, I cracked mine open to read: "Leave all your old troubles behind tonight." You can't make this stuff up.

When we got home, I looked for something distracting to watch on TV. At 9:02 p.m., my phone rang. It was over. Hospice would be called to declare the time of death. The staff at Mount Sinai would be called.

Around the time I made Mom's funeral arrangements last summer, I also investigated dementia research. I wanted some good to come out of my mother's misery if at all possible, and I was able to enroll her in a study at Mount Sinai. At the appointed time, they would pick up Mom's body, remove her brain for analysis and then deliver her body to the funeral home.

I had given the number to the head nurse at Mom's home. Soon after receiving the first call from the home, I received another call from Mount Sinai offering condolences, gratitude, and a request that I fax a signed release so they could take the body. I also contacted the funeral home to facilitate the transfer. The funeral director I dealt with was very nice.

I slept pretty well, all things considered. In the morning, I rose to deliver the sad news. I sent some emails, posted on Facebook, and made some calls. Then I checked some things online. I looked at Mom's checking account. The last of the money from her long-term care policy had been deposited. The final payment had been issued on April 13 and it hit Mom's account on April 15. I couldn't help but grin. At last, I understood why Mom had held on for so long.

Dad wasn't going to let her cross over until she used every last cent of the benefit money from her policy. "Okay Rozzy, you put it to those bastards! Get in the limo! We're going home."

There will be no funeral. There aren't many people who would come. Mom was the youngest of four children who all went before her. The only family remaining are my brother and his clan, Bob and me and our friends. So we'll have a few parties to remember the good times with Roz and Herb, because, truly, all the best times involved them together, as a unit.

I'll look at the pictures, scrub through the videos. I'll weave together a tribute. And I'll finally take a vacation, knowing that I don't have to wait for the dreaded phone call. I got it. It's done.

Mom's body will be cremated and I'll have the remains in five days or so. Next year, we'll bring the ashes to Barnegat Bay, where Roz and Herb began their retirement and had such great times. We'll toast the two of them, reunited with the many family members on the other side, and ponder the change of the guard. We'll laugh and we'll grieve.

Mostly, I feel pretty good. I am sad, but I'm relieved. I'm tired, but optimistic. I'm in the middle of my own journey, certainly closer to the end than the beginning, but I've got a pretty good handle on what's next. I look forward to a peaceful interval, followed by eventual turmoil with a heaping side of fun and gratification.

It sure is good to be off the roller coaster. For now.

EPILOGUE

April 14, 2017

Herb and Roz as I'd prefer to remember them

Mom's been gone two years now. We brought her ashes to Barnegat Bay on the anniversary of her passing. It was a rainy day in April. My four nephews came down with my brother and sister-in-law. They got a look at the house where my folks had lived at the beginning of their retirement. It looks the same as it did when they lived there in the '90s. They'd done so much to make it their own. New owners couldn't do much more to improve it.

On a little beach at the end of the development, my brother read some words he'd prepared. He did a nice job. Then Bob dispensed Mom's ashes into the bay. Some day, perhaps they'll commingle with the ashes of Dad's, deposited in the Intracoastal back in 2005.

We went to a little restaurant on Route 9 and had lunch. I know Herb and Roz would've liked it.

My brother and I have never been close, but we are certainly closer. We are the elders now. It's up to us to maintain continuity, to provide a family framework for the kids and the grandchildren they will have some day.

Our little family has a new member. In September 2015, we adopted a twelve-year-old Yorkie named Penny. Everyone loves her. She's super smart, very funny, well-trained, and adorable.

My mother would have chastised me for taking in such an old dog, and that she would certainly break my heart by dying soon.

And then she would have spoiled the crap out of her and overfed her to the point of exploding.

Last August, our beloved Max took a sudden turn. He had cancer and we had to put him to sleep. He was only twelve and losing him was a shock.

We marked our twenty-fifth wedding anniversary in October by taking that trip to Italy. It was the vacation of a lifetime.

In November 2016, we adopted Fletcher, a very sweet young cat who loves us and adores Penny. Penny clearly dislikes him, but tolerates his presence and affection (at least once she's asleep).

Caregiving came back to claim me on my husband's behalf. New Year's Day 2017, he was hospitalized for a major health crisis, including gout, a staph infection, atrial fibrillation, osteomyelitis, and a host of cross-complicating illnesses. As one of my clients noted, I became a client of my own once again.

Bob is almost fully recovered, and has returned to work in May. This was a challenge I was uniquely qualified to meet.

Meanwhile, I continue to build my business[43] based on what I've learned to help others plan for and cope with the kinds of crises I have endured. There are hundreds of thousands of people about to get on that boat. I hope, for their sake, they have someone like Herby to steer them to the other side.

---

[43] Come visit and learn more at GrandFamilyPlanning.com.

LESSONS LEARNED:
ARTICLES TO GET FAMILIES STARTED ON THEIR PATH

Eight Topics You Must Discuss

One of the toughest things a parent must summon the nerve to address is "the facts of life." Talking to one's children about sex is difficult for most, and it's not exactly fun to hear either. I personally received a lot of misinformation from my peers, which inspired my mother to awkwardly deliver some guidelines and expectations (mostly via books published by a well-known manufacturer of women's hygiene products).

In time, as parents age and their kids start noticing their parents' decline, the next tough discussion will have to come up, one way or another. It's far better to start when your parents are still relatively healthy, competent, and cooperative. Waiting until they're unfit to act on their own behalf is a poor strategy. It will likely be left to you to bring up "the facts of age," so to speak.

Be prepared for pushback. After a lifetime of doing things a particular way, parents are often reluctant to discuss difficult topics with their adult children. No matter how accomplished you are in life, you are still your parents' baby. Be ready to be repelled, but don't be deterred. Seek support from a respected outsider. Having another grown-up in the room goes a long way toward defusing family dynamics.

I've had to learn the hard way. Here's the short list of what really needs to be covered in your tough talk:

1. **Identify all assets**: bank accounts, permanent insurance policies, annuities, properties, cars, boats, anything of value with a title attached. Get signature cards signed. Consider talking to an elder law attorney to make sure you handle your family's situation properly. If you think that's too expensive, talk to someone who's lost everything to a health crisis.

2. **Insurance**: healthcare, long-term care, and life insurance policies. Advisors can help with this. Your parents may be eligible for Medicare, but there's a lot it doesn't cover. Look into supplemental policies and managed Medicare, where the insurer applies the premium allotted for Medicare, and manages care to minimize out of pocket costs. Talking to a broker is free. Long-term care policies are tricky and vary widely. Options continue to evolve as the industry addresses the need. Investigate long-term care strategies with an expert sooner than later.

3. **Formal last will and testament**: Get these done while your parents are competent to review what they have and can still sign legal documents.

4. **Living will** (advance directives): When would they want to pull the plug? It's an extremely important question that needs to be answered formally, in writing, with a lawyer.

5. **Durable power of attorney**: This allows their designee to make financial decisions and sign papers and checks on their behalf if they can't.

6. **Healthcare proxy**: Allows their designees to make health-related decisions for them and gets you past the HIPAA red tape.

7. **Discuss the funeral**: This is really hard, but you need to find out what they're thinking. In the end, funerals are for the benefit of the living, but you'll be sorry if you don't honor what your loved ones really wanted. Funeral homes and other professionals can help you with "pre-need" assessments; you can pre-arrange and prepay, which can be highly beneficial, depending on your family's situation. Shop around, as costs can vary.

8. **Financial and/or estate planning**: Make the most of what your parents have left so you can help them to get through the rest of their lives without fear or hardship (and without having to exhaust your own hard-earned assets). With any luck, there might even be a little something left for you and your kids. Maybe a pizza party? These days, anything left over is a moral victory.

You will no doubt be tempted to put this off indefinitely. Humans tend not to want to confront these difficult issues, especially when your first attempt is met with resistance. But if you wait until your parents begin to show signs of dementia, you could be in for a rougher ride. Months and years slip by quickly, depriving you of choice and opportunity. So if you're reading this and thinking it may be time, it is; don't wait. Time marches on, and that's just another inescapable fact of life.

And once you've addressed your parents' situation, think about your own. One day, your children may be gathering up the courage to have the tough talk with you. Make it easier on them by starting the process sooner. It's one of the most loving gestures you can make.

Please note: This is not meant to be a substitute for advice from professionals. Remember, you get what you pay for, and one small error can cost a lot; the right pros can save you thousands.

COPING STRATEGIES
FOR CARING KIDS

When roles begin to reverse between parents and children, there's bound to be friction. Parents who have always been independent resist the intervention of their kids. Whether it's control, not wishing to be a burden, or a combination, the need to involve one's children is generally uncomfortable. It's natural for children to back down, respecting long-established familial roles. But I've learned some tricks you may find useful in dealing with the transition.

Desired change: hired help in your parent's home.

Parental response: "I don't need a babysitter."

Adult child strategy 1: Make it about *your* needs, not theirs. "Of course you don't need a 'babysitter.' But I would feel better knowing you had a little extra help around the house. I worry about you. If I know someone is coming in to help you, *I'll feel better*. Please, do it for *me*."

Adult child strategy 2: Make it about *extending their independence.* "By having someone come in to help, you can continue to live in *your home* instead of a *facility.* I know you love your place, and this way, you can stay where you are longer."

Desired change: taking away the car keys.

Parental response: "I've been driving for sixty years. Who the hell are you to tell me I can't drive?"

Adult child strategy: This is a terrible thing to have to address, but there comes a time when you know your parent is a danger behind the wheel. Hurting themselves would be bad enough. Potentially hurting others is a catastrophe waiting to happen. Take the keys away from them and sell their car. Give it away to charity if you have to. And if driving them around does not fit your schedule, look for a hired caregiver who can drive them where they need to go. Taxis are another viable option. And if you have to, get the local police involved to revoke their license. This is really hard and painful, but recognizing the danger and allowing your parent to possibly kill or maim others is far worse.

Desired change: the move to a facility.

Parental response: "You are *not* going to warehouse *me.*"

Adult child strategy: Do your homework. Start looking at places *by yourself* before you introduce the idea to your parent. Put yourself in their position. How would *you* like living there? Use checklists of considerations to evaluate facilities objectively. Have a meal or two to see how the food is. Talk to residents and family members. Consider how often you would be able to visit. No matter how great the place is, care will be better when staff knows family may pop in at any time.

When you think you've found a good fit, invite your parent to visit. Realize that they're going to push back until they're ready. Concentrate on the future and setting positive expectations for the transition. When I brought my mom to one place, we chatted with a community relations person, and I told her that what my mother wanted was for me to build a machine that would send her back in time fifteen years. Mom looked at me in awe. "You're right! That *is* what I want." That conversation opened the door for a discussion of an achievable future and how we might look ahead to an exciting new chapter rather than dwelling on sadness and loss.

Realize that this is a *process*. Change is not easy for anyone, and you need to take control of what you can control: the way *you* respond. When you are stepping up, you are doing something noble and valuable. But don't expect gratitude, especially in the beginning. There will be denial, resentment, confusion, and anger. Paranoia, distrust, and misunderstandings are usually part of the package as well. People who were once rational and loving can become delusional and hateful. There's no way to prepare for the emotional impact of these changes. But as you confront your own family transition, do reach out. Seek support, ask for help, talk to professionals. And *don't wait*. Procrastination is human, but it will bite you. Time marches on, and it's much easier to prepare while everyone is still relatively healthy. Keep that strategy in the forefront of your mind and be ready with the others when the need one day arises.

SEVEN HABITS OF DOOMED CAREGIVERS

In my ongoing quest to be productive, the powerful Stephen Covey classic book *The 7 Habits of Highly Effective People* has become a key component of my reference library. The principles outlined make so much sense, I feel as if everyone should know them already. In reality, few embrace proactive and effective living. This knowledge comes, in part, from my membership in the caregiver community.

Family caregivers are some of the nicest, most sincere, hard-working, and generous souls on the planet. They are also some of the least healthy, most angry, and stressed out people who draw breath. I am often frustrated by the things they say and do, because they are quite clearly destroying themselves. Too many of them die young. Many more injure themselves permanently and wind up needing care (too often without the necessary resources or plans in place to enable their own adequate care).

To drive the point home, I offer *The 7 Habits of Doomed Caregivers*:

1. Always do exactly what your loved one asks as soon as they ask no matter how unreasonable it might seem. After all, they are your _____ (fill in the blank: mother, father, grandparent, and so forth) and they always knew best (at least once upon a time).

2. Do everything yourself. No one else cares enough and nobody can do it all as well as you can, right?

3. Never take a day off. You're strong. You can handle it. Your loved one can't go on like this forever, can they? Maybe it just seems like forever.

4. Never ask for help. People will only let you down. If you ask and they say "no," it will only make things more awkward. If they say "yes," they won't do what they promise. Or they'll make you sorry you asked.

5. Don't see your doctors. It's hard enough getting your loved one to their doctors, so you don't have to go for your own visits. Who has the time? You'll be fine. Until you aren't.

6. Don't vent. People will think you're crazy. Or weak. Or exaggerating. So hold it in (until you can't and explode).

7. Give up doing everything you enjoy in order to spend the maximum amount of time with your loved one and to save as much money as you can. Life is short but seems much longer when you don't have any fun, ever.

I see people making these terrible decisions all the time. And there's no payoff, no good reason for it. They usually have options; they just choose the wrong ones out of some misguided idea that the old rules somehow still apply. *They don't.*

Once a loved one becomes ill and you are in charge, *take charge*. If you are caregiving a parent, once you start paying their bills and taking responsibility for your parent's life, you must also have *authority*. If mom or dad make unreasonable demands, your lifelong programming will compel you to comply. But you must learn to fight the impulse. Because what they think *now* is generally irrelevant. They are failing. They are frightened. They want control. But they are no longer capable. You need to take control. That's not easy, but it's essential, for their survival and yours. You are the adult in charge now. You have the experience, strength and perspective to make the best decisions. They no longer do.

And if you need help, ask for help. Hire professionals, and educate yourself as to the resources available.

Facing caregiving alone, and following the seven habits outlined above, is a recipe for disaster. Please don't succumb. Life is too short to be squandered on reckless caregiving. Be more effective and proactive. Develop a team. You have the right to live your own life, on your own terms. It's a shift you can make happen if you have the will. Use your strength wisely.

ACKNOWLEDGMENTS

There would be no *Dementia Sucks* book without the loving support of the following people:

Herb Lawrence, my beloved father. He taught me how to laugh when life got tough. "No one said it was gonna be easy." It's not. But it's worth it. And I'm forever grateful to have earned his friendship, and for all the smart things he did before he got sick.

Rosalind Lawrence, my mother and "star" of *Dementia Sucks*. I never knew her true genius until she started losing her mind. I miss many versions of her.

Bob Bruning, my husband, who said from the very first time I asked that my parents were more than welcome to stay in our home, saying, "They gave me the greatest gift I ever received: their daughter." Now say "awwww."

My brother, Seth, who will probably never talk to me again *if* he reads this. He won't, unless we publish the Cliff Notes, so I'm safe. Love you, bro.

My chosen brother, Glenn Rosenstein, who continues, after all these years, to check in on me as he builds his empire and encourages me to keep building mine. It's amazing how we can still make each other laugh over the dumbest, crudest, silliest stuff imaginable.

Aileen Rabizadeh, also known as "Julia Roberts." She is my business partner, friend, teacher, and my sister. In her mind, this book was written long ago, but if she hadn't gently cajoled me, it might not have been.

Jessica Lomasson, my dear niece. Her reading of the first draft and her ensuing response convinced me that this book had a much broader audience than the one I had originally envisioned. She has always been honest with me and tremendously encouraging. I adore her (and her glorious twin sisters!). I am immensely proud of her and thrilled to be part of her exciting and delightfully creative life. It's awesome when kids you knew as infants grow up to become your friends and people who give you hope for the future of the planet.

Violette Essman, my divine yoga teacher, who is proof of the rejuvenating nature of yoga practice. I would be a different person without her guidance. The affection she has for her students and the support she has shown for my pursuits nourish my soul and bring me great peace.

Debby Englander, my "Book Shepherd." Through a miracle of modern communications, I found her, sent her the draft, and we spoke. Twenty days later, she sent me the contract for the publication you hold in your hands. I can't thank her enough for believing in the book, understanding my objectives, and helping to deliver this volume to the world.

Kathleen Culevier Puig, my singing teacher, who saw me hiding in the shadows and coaxed me into the light. I would not be the confident, capable person I am without her intervention. (And I wouldn't have the respectable vocal range I still possess either.)

Mrs. Edna Meisel, my seventh-grade English teacher, who taught me grammar and wrote in my yearbook, "Keep up the creative writing. You write like a dream." God bless you, Mrs. M.

ABOUT THE AUTHOR

Tracey and Penny

Tracey S. Lawrence was born in 1958 and raised in Brooklyn, New York. Her mother, Rosalind, was a "homemaker" and her father, Herby, owned "taverns."

Excelling in academics and fine arts, Tracey graduated from NYU with a Bachelor of Arts with honors in Psychology at the age of twenty.

She worked as a PBX telephone operator at Macy's Herald Square and as a marketing assistant at a Japanese travel agency in Rockefeller Center (which afforded her the opportunity to travel to the Orient as a tour escort at twenty-two). She also worked for a small advertising agency and found her way into the graphic arts industry as a typographer. She worked at the leading type shops in New York until the demise of the industry in the 1990s.

Acquiring desktop publishing and production skills, she eventually started her own company, Graphic Detail, Inc. Creating artwork, brand identity pieces, websites, and more, her problem-solving nature led her to continue learning. She taught professionals and undergraduates best practices in file creation with her real-world experience.

When her father got sick in 2003, Tracey took on whatever tasks were necessary to help her family cope. Herby died of congestive heart failure (and many other ailments, including dementia) in 2004.

In 2005, Tracey enrolled in a challenging program at NYU and received her Master of Science in Digital Imaging and Design in 2007. She learned video editing, animation, and broadcast design. She serves her town in northern New Jersey by running their public access TV station.

Tracey and her husband, Robert "Big Bob" Bruning, have been married since 1991 and have lived in Ringwood, New Jersey, since 2002. Together they provided ongoing care and support for Tracey's mother, Rosalind, as she tried to live independently in Hallandale Beach, Florida. They brought her into their home as her condition deteriorated. Rosalind died on April 14, 2015, on her sixty-fourth wedding anniversary.

Caring for Rosalind gave Tracey a unique perspective on caregiving, keeping a journal in the form of a blog in order to help others learn from her experiences. Her observations formed the basis of this book.

The team Tracey assembled to help with her mother became the core of her new company, Grand Family Planning LLC. Seeking to take some of the stress out of preparing families for their journeys, she is focused on education, outreach, and provision of coordinated services to enable families to protect themselves from the ravages of a system unequipped for the coming tidal wave of aging, needful people.

Tracey is also a classically-trained rock singer, most recently having performed with a cover band called *Just Play*, with her husband, Bob, on bass and vocals. Their adorable Yorkie, Penny, and their sweet cat, Fletcher, complete their little family. They also enjoy spending time with their nieces, Danielle, Erica, and Jessica, and their respective significant others, as well as Tracey's brother, Seth, and his wife, Teresa, and nephews Alex, Greg, Jonny, Michael, and their dog, Lola.

CONNECT WITH TRACEY ON SOCIAL MEDIA

Tracey S. Lawrence is the founder of Grand Family Planning.
The website is: http://www.grandfamilyplanning.com
Email: traceyslawrence@gmail.com
Facebook Page for "Dementia Sucks": http://
www.facebook.com/DementiaSux/
Twitter: @DementiaBook

6/15/2022
TM